ABSOLUTE POWER

John Hagee

ABSOLUTE POWER

UNLOCK POTENTIAL – FULFILL YOUR DESTINY

JOHN HAGEE

GOOSE CREEK
PUBLISHING

Dedicated to my mother,
Vada Swick Hagee

Never doubt that the power
of a committed prayer life
can change the world.

CONTENTS

INTRODUCTION

It's dark out there.

If you had any doubt that our world is broken and fallen, a glance around should relieve you of all uncertainty.

Thus, it's no surprise that many of God's people are overwhelmed, pessimistic, and despondent. Some have lost hope and given in to despair. But I have written this book to assure you, that is not the appropriate mindset for a child of God. Believers have been given the power to turn things around — for ourselves, for our families, for our communities, and for America.

I'm talking about heavenly power. Divine power. Supernatural power that changes circumstances and destinies. Power that turns the fate of nations. This book, Absolute Power, reveals the various forms this extraordinary force takes. I'll also help you learn to harness and release that power. As you do, supernatural things will happen. That's what this book is all about: discovering and releasing the supernatural power of God in your life.

Two-thousand years ago, there lived on Earth a man named Jesus who was the literal Son of the living God. He raised the dead, He healed the blind, the lame, and the deaf; He touched the rotting flesh of lepers and healed them. Jesus calmed the violent winds and waves and walked on the waters of the sea of Galilee.

He ordered demons to come out with a word. He did not interview them or scream at them all night. He spoke a Word and they obeyed. He fed multitudes with a boy's sack lunch and there was enough left over to start a Jewish delicatessen. He turned water into wine at the wedding in Cana. Jesus spoke with such authority that the politically correct crowd was stunned with silence. The last day of His life, He willingly climbed on His blood-soaked cross on the hills of Calvary and conquered death, hell, and the grave.

The Gospel of Jesus Christ is the Gospel of Power. Saint Paul said in 1 Corinthians 4:20, "For the kingdom of God is not in word, but in power" (KJV). David said in Psalm 62:11, "Power belongs to God."

There is power in His Word. There is power in His blood. There is power in His name. There is power in His presence and in His presence is fullness of joy (see Psalm 16:11). Where is Jesus now? He is seated at the right hand of the Father, which is the position of power in heaven. How is He coming back? With power and great glory in the clouds of heaven.

Jesus said in Matthew 28:18, "All power is given unto me in heaven and in earth" (KJV). Because He possessed the power, Jesus also had the authority to bestow that power onto others: "Then He called His twelve disciples together and gave them power and authority over all demons, and to cure diseases" (Luke 9:1). Jesus looked at his followers and said, "greater works than these he [those who believe] will do" (John 14:12).

The early Church laid hands on the sick and they recovered — That's power! If the pastor of an average mainline American church today were to call for a deliverance service to cast out demon spirits next Sunday, his church board would have him committed.

Ananias and Sapphira, lied about how much money they gave to God, and they were struck dead at the Wednesday night prayer meeting — That's power!

People were attracted to the New Testament Church because of its power. The church experienced daily revivals. They were healing the sick. They were casting out demons. They were winning the lost. They were going from house to house having fellowship and favor with God and man. They were also being persecuted, fed to lions, burned at the stake, and crucified, and through it all . . . they praised God.

If we had that kind of spiritual purity and power in America's churches, there wouldn't be enough funeral homes to handle the dead people next week. If you lived in the New Testament standard of holiness, and you joined the average American church, you would have to backslide to be in fellowship with a majority of the membership.

The early Church thrived under persecution. Peter and John were forbidden to preach in Jesus' name. But unlike some of today's leaders, instead of praying for diplomacy, instead of having seminars on diversity and inclusion, instead of trying to placate hell's legions with political correctness, Peter and John prayed for more boldness.

I assure you; the New Testament church did not deny the inerrancy of the Word of God. They did not deny the virgin birth of Jesus Christ. They did not stop preaching Jesus Christ, and Him crucified. They did not replace the power of the Gospel with some watered down, think-positive message that will never remove the stench of sin from the human soul. When Paul was in jail, beaten for preaching the Gospel, he prayed, not for a more subtle, subdued way to present the Gospel, but for more boldness.

The early Church met demon powers in Philippi and Ephesus head on. They were not afraid to take authority through the power of the Spoken Word of God. If you think the pews of America's churches are not filled with demonized congregations, I have some beachfront property in the Mojave Desert I'll sell you.

In the book of Acts, the Bible says of the early Church: "These who have turned the world upside down..." (Acts 17:6). When the pagans saw Christians coming, that's how they described them — world-changers.

Today's church has stopped setting the world on fire. We stopped walking in the footsteps of our Lord and Savior Jesus Christ and traded Him in for a cotton candy theology that is more New Age than New Testament. We stopped living in God's power and started acting like defeated victims.

Listen! It is God's will for believers to walk in power; supernatural power, healing power, delivering power, power to pull down strongholds, power to break the chains of misery and deadly addictions that enslave some of the people who are reading this right now. You have the power to overcome the world, the flesh and the devil.

It is God's will for his children to know the power of hope, the power of their potential, the power of forgiveness, the power to get wealth, the power of communication, the power of the mind, the power of two, the power of the Word, the power of the Holy Spirit, and the power of the Blood.

It is time that we fill our churches with Spirit-filled congregations who believe in the power of the Gospel. Power is still available to those who will believe it, receive it and release it.

Do you want to see this miracle working power released into your life? Then read on!

ONE

THE POWER OF HOPE

"There is something profound about hope, something so meaningful when you cling to what is beyond anything you know and understand. When that happens deep in your head and in your heart, something shifts. Hope heals." –KATHERINE AND JAY WOLF[1]

"As long as there is life there is hope."
–RABBI LAWRENCE A. HOFFMAN QUOTING THE TALMUD[2]

Hope. All good things begin with it. Thomas Merton once said, "Supernatural hope is the virtue that strips us of all things in order to give us possession of all things."[3] So, it is appropriate that we begin our journey into a supernatural life with an exploration of the extraordinary power of *hope*.

God released the power of hope on Creation morning when He breathed the breath of life into Adam and man became a living soul. After the fall, the battle between good and evil, war and peace, love and hate, and hope and despair, engulfed humanity until this very day. And the enemy will have you believe that there is no hope for tomorrow.

Remember this truth: The saddest, bleakest places on earth are those in which the flickering candle of hope has been snuffed out.

However, no matter how dim your situation is, God has given us a very special gift to help us through our darkest days . . . it is the power of hope. Each day arrives bearing its own gifts, but you must first undo the ribbon. There comes a moment when you must declare that the season of fear and worry are over and now is the time of hope.

What is the driving force in the core of your being that motivates you to achievement or threatens to destroy you? What are your plans for your future? Do you have hope for tomorrow?

Psychologist William Marston asked three-thousand people, "What do you have to live for?" He was shocked to discover that ninety-four percent were simply enduring the present while waiting for something in the future . . . waiting for something to happen . . . waiting for tomorrow . . . waiting for "next year" . . . unable to see that all anyone ever has is today. Yesterday is gone and tomorrow is not a guarantee.[4] We should live the abundant life Today! "This is the day the Lord has made; we shall rejoice and be glad in it (Psalm 118:24).

Have you given up on the key people in your life? Do you live in a prison of bitterness whose bars were created by the vicious words and deeds of others? Have you lost your job, your marriage or a loved one? Are you living without hope?

It's time to recover your hope! It is the golden key that opens the door to heal your heart, mind and soul. Hope has the power to bring joy to a life saturated with pain and suffering. Ecclesiastes 9:4 declares that, "Anyone who is among the living has hope." Hope achieves the impossible. It can revive, inspire and empower you. Hope is the companion of power and the mother of success.

I've never forgotten the lesson in tenacious hope I learned in the story of a remarkable woman born in Massachusetts in 1836. Rendered nearly blind by a bacterial infection at the age of five, "Little Annie" was orphaned when she was only eight and sent to the infamous Tewksbury Hospital — a combination of poor-house and an insane asylum.

There, Little Annie was locked up in what was essentially a dark dungeon. This was the only appropriate place, said the doctors, for someone so hopelessly broken. In Little Annie's case, they saw no hope for her, so she was consigned to a living death in a small cage, with little light, and even less reason for hope.

About that time, an elderly nurse nearing retirement took an interest in Annie's case. Compelled by the conviction that there is hope for all God's children, she started taking her lunch into the dungeon and eating it outside the child's cage once each week. She felt perhaps she could communicate love to the little girl.

In many ways, Annie was like an animal. On occasion, she would violently attack the person who came within her reach. At other times, she would ignore a visitor completely. When the elderly nurse started visiting her, Annie gave no indication that she was aware of her presence.

One day, the elderly nurse brought some brownies to the dungeon and left them outside the cage. When the nurse returned the next day, the brownies were gone. From that time on, the nurse would bring brownies when she made her weekly visit.

These regular visits ignited in Annie a spark of something utterly vital to the human soul: hope.

Soon thereafter, the doctors in the institution noticed positive changes in Annie's condition. Eventually, they decided they should move Annie upstairs to receive more conventional help. Her progress continued steadily until the day came when the "hopeless case" was told she could be released to live her life as best she could. But Annie did not wish to leave. She chose to stay and join the staff, to help others climb out of the same dark pit of despair she had known.

Ultimately, it was she, Miss Anne Sullivan, who came to care for, teach, and nurture a little blind and deaf girl named Helen Keller.[5]

This is the power of hope. Hope sees the invisible, feels the intangible, and achieves the impossible. Yet there are additional dimensions of the power of hope to explore.

HOPE: THE MOTHER OF SUCCESS

Our fallen world is unpredictable. You can be sailing along blissfully on the sea of life, the waters calm, and the sky a beautiful blue. There is a slight breeze and life is good. Then it happens. Pow! Like lightning from a clear blue sky at noonday, trouble strikes. The unthinkable happens.

One day, a marriage can seem rock solid. The next day, one spouse discovers that the other has had a secret lover for months. He or she wants a divorce. Children will be collateral damage. The elements of a shared life are suddenly scattered like debris in a tornado.

What a difference a day can make!

A trip to the doctor's office is just another routine annual physical check-up until an X-ray reveals something that should not be there. The drive home is filled, not with thoughts of to do lists and projects, but of death and how our loved ones will be impacted.

On a quiet evening, the phone rings and it's the voice of a police officer saying your teenager has been involved in a major car crash. Parents race to the hospital and see the battered body of their precious child surrounded by doctors fighting to save her. Life will never be the same.

After years of faithful service to a corporation, an employee goes to work one beautiful morning and sees a cadre of executives huddled together in the president's office. Later, he's told the firm is downsizing and his position no longer exists. Your financial future is shattered. Your dreams for a comfortable retirement are gone.

What do you do if you find yourself is such a situation? King David gives the answer: ". . . hope thou in God" (Psalm 42:5, KJV).

Hope is the anchor of the soul that holds life together until the storm passes.

The following story of a severely burned Israeli tank commander in the Yom Kippur War of 1973 is told by Rebbetzin Esther Jungreis:

We entered a room in which the light had been dimmed. The patient lay immobile in his bed, wrapped in bandages like a mummy. Rebbetzin greeted the wounded warrior with, "Shalom to you, my name is Esther Jungreis. We came from the States to bring you greetings and blessings." There was no answer. "What is your name?" Rebbetzin asked. Still the wounded warrior did not respond. The nurse explained that he had been badly burned in a tank battle on the Golan. Rebbetzin greeted the tanker again, stating she had brought a little token, a symbol of blessing, and held up the medallion.

For the first time, the young soldier spoke: "Take your medallion; it's of no use to me!"

"I understand that you are hurting but I'm going to leave it on the night table anyway. You might just need it one day," responded Rebbetzin.

"Need it for what?" came the angry answer.

"For an engagement gift," she responded.

The wounded warrior let out a bitter laugh. "Who would want to marry me? I'm a vegetable. No one will ever marry me."

"It will happen. You are never allowed to give up hope. You will see that in time you will meet a girl, and when you do you must tell her that a Rebbetzin from the United States visited you and told you that you have a special merit before God, that you are ready to transmit that merit to her, and this medallion is a symbol of that."

The warrior responded, "Rebbetzin, if I said that to any girl, she would think I'm crazy."

"You're wrong. Some place, somewhere, there is one girl who will understand, and you only need one," she responded.

A year later the Rebbetzin returned to Israel and her first stop was an army recuperation center near Haifa. It is a tradition in Israel to present guest speakers and artists with a bouquet of flowers. At the conclusion of her program, a soldier in a wheelchair was brought up on stage to make the presentation.

"Do you recognize me, Rebbetzin?" he asked.

"You look familiar," she said. "Please help me out."

He smiled and pointed to the nurse standing behind his wheelchair. "I would like you to meet my wife." She had the medallion around her neck.[6]

Hope achieves the impossible! In what area of your life is hope fading or gone? Revive it! Hope is the companion of power and the mother of success. "Anyone who is among the living has hope . . ." (Ecclesiastes 9:4, NIV).

HOPE IS GOD'S GIFT TO THE BELIEVER

Saint Paul puts pen to parchment and addresses the people of God — and you — proclaiming that we are to abide in faith, hope, love. (1 Corinthians 13:13)

The prophet Jeremiah communicates the heart of God for you when he writes: "'For I know the plans I have for you,' declares the LORD. 'They are plans for good and not for disaster, to give you a future and a hope'" (Jeremiah 29:11, NLT).

God put you on this earth for a specific purpose. The great Architect of the Universe has a plan for you, which He has never assigned to another. You have a heaven-born, divine destiny with unlimited potential. The favor of the Father is at work in your future, above and beyond your wildest dreams.

That favor is better than silver or gold. The favor of God is more to be prized than houses and lands. The favor of God is far superior to the applause of prime ministers and presidents. One day of favor from the throne of God can reverse a lifetime of pain, suffering.

Consider Joseph, the favorite son of Jacob. His coat of many colors, the bold, visible symbol of favoritism from his father, inflamed hatred in his eleven brothers. They so completely hated Joseph that they refused to speak to him. When Jacob sent Joseph to the fields with food for his brothers, they mocked him as he approached. They threw him into a pit and plotted how they would explain his death to their father, Jacob.

As you probably know, a band of Midianite traders happened by at the critical moment, and instead of being murdered, Joseph was sold into slavery. The Midianites took Joseph to Egypt and sold him a second time into slavery at Potiphar's house. History refers to this exceptional young man as "Beautiful Joseph."

Potiphar's "desperate housewife" tried to seduce Joseph, but he spurned her. In anger, she falsely accused him of sexual assault, and he was sent to prison for years in Egypt. Joseph endured twelve years of living hell, but after every tragic reversal, the Word of God clearly states: "the LORD was with him" (see Genesis 39:2, 23).

God continued to be with Joseph. He was with Joseph when the warden put him in charge of all the prisoners. God was with Joseph when two imprisoned officials needed an interpreter for their dreams. The Lord was with Joseph when no one else could interpret Pharaoh's dreams. The Most High was with Joseph when Pharaoh made him second in command over the palace. And God was with Joseph when his brothers showed up looking for food in a time of famine.

In a single day, Beautiful Joseph went from the living hell of the Egyptian penitentiary to the luxury and power of Pharaoh's penthouse. In a day, he went from being a prisoner to the most powerful person in Egypt, save Pharaoh himself.

The favor of God on Joseph saved an entire nation of Gentiles from starvation through his prophetic understanding that seven years of severe famine would immediately follow seven years of abundance. Pharaoh gave Joseph and his extended family — which at that time was seventy in number — the fertile farming lands of Goshen. Here, the Jewish people over the course of three-hundred and forty years became a great nation. A nation that would ultimately be led out by Moses to the land of promise. A nation that would produce Jesus Christ of Nazareth, a nation who would write every book of the Bible and bless the world.

What made that extraordinary chain of events possible? It happened because Joseph never gave up on the hope he had in Jehovah, and his God rewarded him with levels of favor the world remembers to this day. What a gift hope is to the child of God!

Are you having a bad day? When you are tempted to mount your pity pot and start rehearsing all the bad things that have happened to you lately, take time to remember Joseph and how his hope in God delivered him from his accusers and made him the prince of the world.

Did someone get your parking place at the church? Was someone sitting in your pew when you arrived? Was the auditorium too cold or the music too loud? Did the preacher preach too long? Did he look at you too often? Or not enough? This is not the Great Tribulation; press on! See yourself as clean and bright because you are the window through which you will see the world.

Hope produces a joy the world cannot give and cannot take away. Hope produces a song that sings in the midnight hour in the jail at Philippi when Paul and Silas had been beaten bloody by Roman whips for preaching the Gospel of Jesus Christ. Hope is faith reaching out in the darkness knowing the God we serve never fails. Saint Paul said in his darkest hour of trial: ". . . we rejoice in hope of the glory of God" (Romans 5:2, ESV).

These words remind us that Joseph is not our only biblical exemplar of hope in action.

HOPE FOR THE BROKENHEARTED

The Apostle Paul, the midwife to the newborn New Testament Church, a Jewish believer of the Tribe of Benjamin who wrote most of the New Testament, was hopeful despite unspeakable suffering and persecution. Listen to Paul describe his life:

> *. . . in labors more abundant, in stripes above measure,*
> *in prisons more frequently, in deaths often. From*
> *the Jews five times I received forty stripes minus one.*
> *Three times I was beaten with rods; once I was stoned;*

*three times I was shipwrecked; a night and a day
I have been in the deep; in journeys often, in perils
of waters, in perils of robbers, in perils of my own
countrymen, in perils of the Gentiles, in perils in the
city, in perils in the wilderness, in perils in the sea, in
perils among false brethren; in weariness and toil, in
sleeplessness often, in hunger and thirst, in fastings
often, in cold and nakedness — besides the other
things, what comes upon me daily: my deep concern
for all the churches.* (2 Corinthians 11:23–28, NKJV)

Paul was actually understating his trials. He doesn't even mention being bitten by vipers in Malta or led outside the city of Rome to be decapitated. And you and I feel persecuted because someone failed to speak to us last Sunday morning! We feel abused because the secular media has criticized our church or pastor for his Bible preaching?

Today's hot tub, comfort-demanding Christians find it difficult to grasp the agony and the suffering cheerfully endured by our spiritual forefathers. When they gathered for worship, they were thankful some of their members had not been fed to the lions for the amusement of Caesar and his demented legions.

Listen as Saint Paul commands our generation to: "rejoice in hope of the glory of God" (Romans 5:2, NKJV) and "Be joyful in hope . . ." (Romans 12:12, NIV).

Paul admonishes our generation to behave like Christians: "Let love be without hypocrisy. Abhor what is evil. Cling to what is good. Be kindly affectionate to one another with brotherly love, in honor giving preference to one another" (Romans 12:9–10, NKJV).

We have forgotten in our self-centered, cell-phone-addicted society how committed Christians were to each other in the first century. We have forgotten the public display of affection they had toward one another — not just in their greeting to each other, but Paul admonished the Church to, "Greet one another with a holy kiss" (Romans 16:16, NKJV). That's off the charts for our churches today.

Have you ever considered the power of a hug to someone with a broken heart? How many times in my sixty plus years of ministry have I walked into a home where the grief was so deep, hearts were so broken, and tears were without measure. There are no words in human speech to heal a broken heart, but I have found simply hugging someone shaken and sobbing in sorrow is a healing force.

Medical science is now saying hugs are healthy. Hugs can boost the immune system, improve your mood, and lower blood pressure.[7] Hugs are invigorating, rejuvenating, and have no unpleasant side effects. Hugging is being called a miracle drug. Hugging is all natural. It is organic, naturally sweet, with no artificial ingredients, and is one-hundred percent wholesome. Hugging is the ideal gift! Great for any occasion, fun to give and receive, shows you care, comes with its own wrapping, and is fully returnable. When we open our hearts and our arms, we encourage others to do the same.

Think of the people in your life. When the pain of life is unbearable, when words are too feeble to heal the grief, hugs carry the healing power of hope.

HOPE IS BASED ON SUBSTANCE AND EVIDENCE

"I wish." We all have wishes for ourselves and other people for the future. These wishes are our perception of what we think would be best for us or believe would satisfy us.

When I was a boy living in the country in southeast Texas, my family called the Sears and Roebuck Catalog "The Wish Book". As a six-year-old, I poured through the pages of that catalog at least three times a week wishing for a Daisy Air Rifle. That Christmas, my father gave me what I wished for. He gave me that BB gun. My older brother, Bill, tried to take it away from me on Christmas Day. He was twice my size, so I shot him. Don't worry. I did the Christian thing and merely shot him in the leg.

I can assure you, when my father caught up with me, I was not singing "Joy to the World" but rather remembering that famous sermon of Jonathan Edwards', "Sinners in the Hands of an Angry God."

Fast forward to the twenty-first century, and fully understand that millions of Americans are looking in a "wish book" for our future and selecting the poison of socialism. Socialism is a fraud! In history, it has never worked. In the past century, it has killed over one-hundred million people under the leadership of socialists like Hitler, Stalin, and Mao.

The Daily Caller reports that one-in-three millennials in America see socialism as favorable, and seventy percent are prepared to vote for a socialist. Why? When we don't educate our younger generation about the historical truth, we shouldn't be surprised at their willingness to embrace the endless promises of socialism, which will be the absolute destruction of the United States of America.

But hope is not wishful thinking. Saint Paul writes, "Now faith is the substance of things hoped for, the evidence of things not seen" (Hebrews 11:1). Hear these two words: "substance" and "evidence." Our hope is based on the "substance" of what God has done in the past and the "evidence" found in the Bible.

God's provisions are in His promises, and they are all found in His Word. If God has done it in the past, He will do it today. Therefore, our hope is based on God's performance knowing that He is faithful to His Word, which accomplishes all He has assigned it to accomplish.

And because of this promise, I don't simply *hope* God answers prayer; I *know* God answers prayer because: Moses prayed to God and the Red Sea parted; Daniel prayed, and God muzzled the mouths of hungry lions, lions that later devoured his enemies; Elijah prayed, and God sent cloven tongues of fire from heaven and consumed the sacrifice being offered on Mount Moriah; John 14: 13 records what Jesus prayed and declared to His followers in every generation, *"Whatsoever ye shall ask in My name, that will I do"* (KJV). Hope is established by the past performance of God: God Almighty answers prayer!

Are you in a major crisis? The Bible promises, "Many are the afflictions of the righteous, but the LORD delivers him out of them all" (Psalm 34:9, ESV). Be of good courage, be bold, be fearless for the Lord our God is with you (see Psalm 31:24; Joshua 1:9). And remember: "If God is for us, who can be against us?" (Romans 8:31).

God Almighty is your fortress, your high tower, your deliverer, your shield and buckler, your eternal source of hope that never fails. The Bible is the most exciting, optimistic, and hopeful manuscript ever written. Where can you read a book that promises boundless love, joy unspeakable, peace that surpasses understanding, prosperity, health, confidence, security, and eternal life? The Bible not only promises . . . it delivers on every promise!

Do you want a severe case of depression? Just turn to the five leading causes of emotional depression in

America: ABC, NBC, CBS, Facebook, and Instagram. On the other hand, if you want to get so excited about life that you injure yourself getting out of bed in the morning, read the Bible. It is the most hopeful and inspiring manuscript God has ever given to mankind.

Through the pages of Scripture, Jesus offers hope for a better life. John 14:6 declares that He is "the way, the truth, and the life." Revelation 22:16 says that He is "the blessed hope that never fails." He is "the Bright and Morning star" that leads us in paths of righteousness that bring unlimited blessings. He is the fairest of ten thousand. He is "the rose of Sharon and the lily of the valleys" (Song of Solomon 2:1). He is heaven's hope and hell's dread. Ezekiel 48:35 proclaims that Jesus is *Jehovah-Shammah*, "THE LORD [WHO] IS THERE."

He is the Husband to the widow and the Father to the orphan. He is the Lamb of God for sinners slain. He is the Lion of the Tribe of Judah, the Light of the World, and the Lord of Glory. He is the God of all hope . . . "hope thou in God" (Psalm 42:11, KJV).

HOPE BRINGS JOY

The story is told of a Baptist deacon who went to his company's business party and, being extremely naïve, drank too much spiked punch. He went home quite drunk and woke up the next morning with a fierce headache. He opened his eyes and saw two aspirin on the nightstand and took them immediately. He went into the bathroom, looked into the mirror, and saw a huge black eye.

There was a note on the mirror from his wife that read, "Sweetheart, your breakfast is on the kitchen table. Two eggs over easy with bacon, toast and jelly. The coffee is hot. I've gone shopping for your favorite foods for supper. Be back soon, your loving wife."

The deacon's son came into the room and the father asked, "Son, what happened last night?"

The boy responded, "Dad, you came home at three a.m. and broke the coffee table when you fell flat on your face. Mom was helping you into the bedroom and you hit the door, which explains your black eye. As mom was pulling off your pants to put you into bed, you started screaming: 'Leave me alone; I'm a married man!'"

The son concluded: "Dad, for breaking the coffee table, five-hundred dollars. For two aspirin, thirty-five cents. For saying the right thing at the right time . . . PRICELESS!"

Joy unspeakable!

If you didn't laugh at that joke, keep reading. This next part is for you.

Saint Paul records in Romans 15:13, "Now may the God of hope fill you with all joy and peace in believing, that you may abound in hope by the power of the Holy Spirit" (NKJV). Joy is the proof of God's presence in your life.

Have you lost your joy? That bird singing outside your window — is it a buzzard? Do you feel the only way you can wake up in the morning with a smile on your face is to go to bed at night with a clothes hanger in your mouth? Is someone always raining on your parade?

I think it's important that we make the distinction between happiness and joy. Happiness comes from the Scandinavian root word "Hap" from which we get the word "happenstance." The essence of this word means that your happiness depends on what happens to you. God's joy, on the other hand, is present no matter what happens to you. That's the difference between "happiness" and "joy."

Americans are searching for joy where they will never find it. They are searching for joy in drugs that are killing our young people by the thousands. Sex trafficking, as evidenced in the sexual empire created by the late Jeffery Epstein and his list of blackmailable global playboys, and mass murders, being committed by demonized slaves of evil who slaughter innocent people at churches, synagogues, public schools, and shopping centers, bear witness of America's moral corruption.

These horrific crimes against humanity cannot be stopped by legislation from Washington D.C. These crimes are a symptom of the moral corruption of our society.

The cure will not come from the top down. It must arise from the bottom up. America did not get in this mess over the weekend, and it will take a national return to righteousness to save this nation.

The American family has disintegrated. Fathers have abandoned their children, and those children have gone into the streets looking for leadership and significance. They are finding it with gangs, drug lords, and anarchists raging in the streets.

We have joyless marriages. Legions of married couples have lost all hope that their marriage can be resurrected from the dead. Every married person reading this book needs to understand that their marriage can be better. There is no such thing as a hopeless marriage. What does a good marriage cost you? Everything you've got! And it's worth it at any cost.

Many marriages are unhappy because neither partner can manage their money. That truth reminds me of the story of Dan. Dan was a single guy living at home with his father and working in the family business. When he found out he was going to inherit five-hundred million dollars when his eighty-five-year-old sickly father died, Dan decided he needed a wife with which to share his fortune.

One evening at an investment seminar, he spotted the most beautiful woman he had ever seen. Her natural beauty took his breath away. He walked across the room, extended his hand and introduced himself, saying, "I may look like an ordinary man, but in a very short time my father will die, and I will inherit five-hundred million dollars." The woman was very impressed. She took his business card and three days later became his stepmother.

I have found in my life that women are great financial planners.

In all seriousness, America is saturated with dysfunctional families. Nearly thirty percent of America's children do not live in a two-parent household.[8] The divorce rate of our nation is off the charts. Mothers and fathers are at war and their children are casualties of the domestic battleground.

Dear reader, you may have come from a dysfunctional family. You may even be in one presently. Is there any hope? Yes!

Let me tell you about one of the most famous families in the world who were absolutely dysfunctional yet changed the course of history. From Genesis 12–50, God portrays this dysfunctional family. These are the highlights that would never have made FOX News because they are too unbelievable. Truth is often more unbelievable than fiction!

Headline: "Husband Gives His Wife to Another Man to Spend the Night." This is the story of Abraham giving his wife Sarah to Abimelech, king of Gerar, telling him she was his "sister" (see Genesis 20:2). Rabbinical schools confirm Abraham knew there would be a sexual encounter in the tent. What's the point? Abraham is called in

Scripture "a friend of God" (James 2:23, NKJV) and "the father of us all [who believe]" (Romans 4:16, ESV). Yes, there is hope for your marriage!

Consider the second dysfunctional family in the book of Genesis. This husband had a wife who was a master manipulator. She helped her favorite son steal the family inheritance from the firstborn son who rightfully should have received it. This is the story of Rebekah instructing Jacob, her favorite son, on how to steal the inheritance of Esau, the older brother. The story ends with Jacob stealing the inheritance and running for his life from his angry brother. He never saw his mother again and the family was fractured forever (see Genesis 27). What's the point? Jacob became a patriarch in Israel. To this day, God is identified as "the God of Abraham, the God of Isaac, and the God of Jacob" (Matthew 22:32, ESV).

Jacob had twelve sons who became the twelve tribes of Israel. Those twelve tribes produced the prophets of the Old Testament and the kings who birthed the nation of Israel, specifically King David. Out of King David, generations later, came Jesus of Nazareth who died on a Roman cross for the redemption from sin for all the world . . . which includes you. Yes, your wayward son can amount to something!

The third illustration of a dysfunctional family in Genesis was the daughter-in-law who disguised herself as a prostitute and seduced her father-in-law in order to get pregnant (see Genesis 38). This is incest! Talk about "Desperate Housewives"!

How's that for a serial family chaos? Almighty God takes thirty-eight chapters to tell the story of this dysfunctional family, in detail, to encourage you. Your family has hope for tomorrow! The statistics may seem hopeless, but when you "hope thou in God" (Psalm 42:11, KJV), the impossible becomes your reality.

AGAINST ALL HOPE

There was a man in ancient Israel who desired above all else to have a son who could carry his name and inherit his wealth. He and his wife tried for years to have a son and could not. Even though the man approached one-hundred years of age and his wife ninety, God promised him he would have a son. That man was Abraham, "the father of us all [who believe]." God promised Abraham that his seed would be as numerous as the stars in the sky and as the sands of the seashore. When Sarah heard the angels, who brought the message that at this time next year she would bear a son, she laughed (see Genesis 18). God kept His promise and a year later, Isaac, "the son of laughter," was born (see Genesis 21). Joy unspeakable!

Saint Paul records Abraham's miracle son and Isaac's miraculous birth in Romans 4:18–19, saying:

. . . who, contrary to hope, in hope believed, so that he became the father of many nations, according to what was spoken, "So shall your descendants be." And not being weak in faith, Abraham did not consider his own body, already dead (since he was about a hundred years old), and the deadness of Sarah's womb. (NKJV)

By all accounts, the situation was hopeless. Yet, against all hope, Abraham continued to hope, because his hope was not in his circumstances. His hope was not in what the world says is possible. His hope was in God. The hope in Abraham gave him the endurance to receive the impossible: a son born to him at age one-hundred and to a wife whose womb was dead.

What is it in your life that you hope for? I ask this question virtually every Sunday morning in the Visitor's Reception at Cornerstone Church. Almost every person, every week, lifts their hand and indicates that there is a deep-seated hope in the depth of their soul that they want from God. Does this describe you? God's hope gives you the endurance to receive His answer for the thing you long for to fulfill your dreams. Hope will give you the endurance to achieve the impossible!

This truth puts me in remembrance of a boy who, against astonishing odds, rode hope and determination to amazing heights of achievement.

THE HOPE OF A CHAMPION

The little country schoolhouse was heated by an old fashioned, pot-bellied coal stove. A little boy had the job of coming to school early each day to start a fire and warm the room before his teacher and classmates arrived.

One morning, they arrived to find the schoolhouse engulfed in flames. They dragged the unconscious little boy out of the flaming building, more dead than alive. He had major burns over the lower half of his body and was taken to the nearby county hospital.

From his bed, the dreadfully burned, semi-conscious little boy faintly heard the doctor talking to his mother. The doctor told his mother that her son would surely die . . . which was for the best. The terrible fire had devastated the lower half of his body.

But the brave boy was a fighter, a warrior! He made up his mind that he would survive. Miraculously, to the amazement of the physician, he did survive. When the mortal danger had passed, he again heard the doctor speaking quietly to his mother stating the fire had destroyed so much flesh in the lower part of his body, it would almost be better if he had died, since he was doomed to be a lifetime cripple with no use of his legs.

Once more, the brave boy made up his mind. He would not give up hope; he would not be a cripple. He would walk. But unfortunately, from his waist down, he had no motor ability. His thin legs just dangled, all but lifeless.

Ultimately, he was released from the hospital. Every day, his mother would massage his tiny legs, but there was no feeling, no control, nothing. Yet, his determination that he would walk was as strong as ever.

When he wasn't in bed, he was confined to a wheelchair. One sunny day, his mother wheeled him out into the yard to get some fresh air. This day, instead of sitting there, in a burst of hope he threw himself from the chair, pulled himself across the grass, dragging his legs behind him.

He dragged his body to the white picket fence bordering their lot. With great effort, he raised himself up on the fence. Then, stake by stake, he began dragging himself along the fence, determined that he would walk.

Driven by hope, he started to do this every day until he had worn a smooth path all around the yard beside the fence. There was nothing he wanted more than to develop life in those legs.

Ultimately, through daily massages, his hopeful persistence, and his resolute determination, he did develop the ability to stand up, then to walk by himself, and then to run.

He began to walk to school, then run to school, and run for the sheer joy of running. Later, in college, he made the track team as a distance runner, specializing in the mile. The fire had burned the nerves in his legs, and he felt no pain as his body raced around the track.

In Madison Square Garden this young man, who was not expected to survive, who would surely never walk, who could never hope to run . . . this determined young man, Dr. Glen Cunningham, ran a mile faster than any person ever had.[9]

Never underestimate the power of hope! The power of hope allows you to believe the unbelievable, bear the unbearable, and achieve the impossible. That isn't true only for biblical heroes, it is true for all who believe and place their hope in God.

THE POWER OF YOUR POTENTIAL

"When the New Testament says, 'The kingdom of God is within you,' (Luke 17:21) it is informing us that God our Creator has laid up within our minds and personalities all the potential powers and ability we need for constructive living. It remains for us to tap and develop these powers." –NORMAN VINCENT PEALE[10]

There is a difference between making a great living and having a great life. Plenty of people make a great living but lead miserable lives, lives that lack peace, joy, and hope.

The Bible says it this way:

A man may have a hundred children and live many years; yet no matter how long he lives, if he cannot enjoy his prosperity and does not receive proper burial, I say that a stillborn child is better off than he. It comes without meaning, it departs in darkness, and in darkness its name is shrouded. Though it never saw the sun or knew anything, it has more rest than does that man — even if he lives a thousand years twice over but fails to enjoy his prosperity. Do not all go to the same place? (Ecclesiastes 6:3–6, NIV).

Yes, that's in the Bible. Solomon, the wisest man who ever lived, believed that it would be better — more peaceful — to be born dead than to not be able to enjoy your own life.

Friend, contrary to what you may have been told, it is possible to be a Christian and still be happy. Many people believe that being spiritual means walking around looking like you've been sucking a lemon all day. But that is not spirituality; that's religious legalism, and legalism is a curse.

But I have good news! Salvation through the blood of Jesus Christ sets you free to serve the Lord of the Bible and enjoy the life He died to give you — a life filled with powerful potential.

Back when Elvis Presley was at the peak of his career, his manager, Colonel Tom Parker, arranged for me to meet and talk with him in his hotel room in San Antonio, Texas. Elvis had everything that money could buy. He had luxury cars. He had jets. He had diamonds. He had fame. He had the applause of fans. He had a telephone that was covered with gold. Yet, I've never met a lonelier person. At the end of our conversation, Elvis said, "Pastor, will you pray for me?" I prayed with him. Elvis was a good person. He had a great living. But he had a hurting heart and a lonely, empty, joyless life.

What kind of life do you have? Are you living with divine purpose? Does your life have meaning? Or are you lonely? Are you angry? Are you frustrated? Are you chasing illusions that never materialize? Is your home in crisis? Is your marriage a war zone? If so, then you are not living up to your powerful potential. You see, God has made it possible for you to have peace that surpasses all understanding. He has made it possible for you to have joy unspeakable and full of glory. He has made it possible for you to experience unconditional love.

The Bible says, ". . . love is of God; and everyone who loves is born of God and knows God. He who does not love does not know God, for God is love" (1 John 4:7–8, NKJV). If you don't have love, you don't know God. I want to tell you, from the depth of my heart, there is a Father in heaven who loves you more than you can possibly imagine. Even if your mother and your father forsake you, Jesus promises that He will never leave you. He will be with you in the darkest valley. Nothing can separate you from His love.

WINGS AS EAGLES

So, what is your potential? The answer to that question is far greater than you believe. Henry Ford once said, "There is no man living who isn't capable of doing more than he thinks he can do."[11]

There is a story in Native American folklore about a Brave who found an eagle's egg and put it in the nest of a prairie chicken. The eaglet hatched with a brood of chicks and grew up thinking he was a prairie chicken. He scratched the dirt for seeds and insects to eat. He clucked and cackled. He flew briefly but always for just a few feet, because that is what prairie chickens do.

Years passed and the earthbound eagle grew into maturity. One day he saw something he had never seen before: a mighty and majestic bird flying in the heavens. He asked his earthbound brothers what it was, "What kind of bird is that?" And the answer came back, "That's an eagle, chief of all birds, but don't get any ideas. You can never be like him." So, the mighty eagle never gave it another thought. He died scratching in the dirt because he thought he was a prairie chicken.

Are you scratching in the dirt, living a shallow and empty life, rather than flying on the wings of faith? Or are you going from one adventure to the next with the grace of God, doing things you thought were absolutely impossible, yet knowing that with God — nothing is impossible!

Isaiah declared, "But they that wait upon the LORD shall renew their strength; they shall mount up with wings as eagles; they shall run, and not be weary; and they shall walk, and not faint" (Isaiah 40:31). Dare to fly on the wings of faith when the cowards around you are scratching in the dirt. Remember: When God is in you, nothing is impossible!

Wouldn't we all love to have a certified letter that cited our highest potential? A document proclaiming that we are more than we think we are, that we can accomplish more than we thought possible, and that we can live a greater life than we are currently living?

We have received that letter and it is called the Word of God. The Bible is a love letter to every believer declaring the power of our potential to live an unlimited life of accomplishment. But you must first read it and then believe it.

You can destroy your potential with negative thinking, or you can reach the fullness of it by believing what God's Word says about you. You are God's masterpiece. You are an ambassador of Christ. You were created to do good works, works meant just for you. God has given you a gift. Find out what it is and do it better than anyone else. You have a life without limit.

King Solomon said, "For as he thinketh in his heart, so is he" (Proverbs 23:7, KJV). Saint Paul said, "whatsoever things are true, whatsoever things are honest, whatsoever things are just, whatsoever things are pure, whatsoever things are lovely, whatsoever things are of good report . . . think on these things" (Philippians 4:8).

What is your potential? What do you see when you look in the mirror? Do you see a person who lacks confidence about the future? Or do you see a person with the call of God on your life? Are you destroying your potential with stinking thinking? Or are you speaking the power of God and the truth of His Word over your life?

Are you fearful about what you think is about to happen? Or are you eagerly anticipating the plans and purposes that God has ordained?

Have you given up on your dream of success? Or are you a person with big dreams depending on an even bigger God, a God who wants to do the impossible in and through you? Has your life become a meaningless treadmill of insignificance? Or do you see yourself as God sees you . . . a person whose potential is limitless?!

FUEL FOR THE IMPOSSIBLE

People react to challenges in life in one of two ways: they either succumb to them and become pity pots; or they use them as fuel to do the impossible, the unimaginable, and go down in history as overcomers.

In 1856, Booker T. Washington was born into slavery. After the end of the Civil War, he became a free person and worked as a janitor to pay for his education. Later he became the first president and principal founder of the Tuskegee Institute, which educated former slaves.

In his book, *My Larger Education*, Washington wrote:

Paradoxical as it may seem, the difficulties that the Negro has met since emancipation have, in my opinion, not always, but on the whole, helped him more than they have hindered him. For example, I think the progress which the Negro has made within less than half a century in the matter of learning to read and write the English language has been due in large part to the fact that, in slavery, this knowledge was forbidden him. My experience and observation have taught me that people who try to withhold the best things in civilization from any group of people, or race of people, not infrequently aid that people to the very things that they are trying to withhold from them. I am sure that, in my own case, I should never have made the efforts that I did make in my early boyhood to get an education and still later to develop the Tuskegee Institute in Alabama if I had not been conscious of the fact that there were a large number of people in the world who did not believe that the Negro boy could learn or that members of the Negro race could build up and conduct a large institution of learning. A wider acquaintance with men in all the different grades of life taught me that the Negro's case is not peculiar. The majority of successful men are persons who have had difficulties to overcome, problems to master; and, in overcoming those difficulties and mastering those problems, they have gained strength of mind and a clearness of vision that few persons who have lived a life of ease have been able to attain. Experience has taught me, in fact, that no man should be pitied because, every day in his life, he faces a hard, stubborn problem, but rather that it is the man who has no problem to solve, no hardships to face, who is to be pitied. His misfortune consists in the fact that he has nothing in his life which will strengthen and form his character; nothing to call out his latent powers and deepen and widen his hold on life.[12]

That was a long quote, so I want to make sure you didn't miss the point of it. Booker T. Washington said he would have never accomplished what he did if it weren't for the fact that he knew people thought it was impossible. He thought that the majority of people who achieve great success "are persons who have had difficulties to overcome." Washington believed that it was precisely because of the adversity he faced in his life that made him a person of character, that forced him to discover "his latent powers" — the power of his potential!

Never underestimate the power of your potential under adversity. In fact, stress and adversity can be the catalyst to propel you into your purpose.

Nick Vujicic was born without arms or legs. Does he spend his days feeling sorry for himself? No! He is an internationally renowned evangelist. He is an author, musician, and actor. He swims and skateboards and speaks to stadiums full of people about the incredible love of God and its power to overcome anything. He has a pair of sneakers in his closet because he believes in the power of God to perform miracles, but he isn't waiting for his miracle to start living a life of purpose. He is a husband and father and the president and CEO of the nonprofit organization, Life Without Limbs. He is living the power of potential every single day.[13]

Joni Eareckson Tada broke her neck in a diving accident in 1967 at the age of seventeen, leaving her a quadriplegic. Has she spent the past fifty years at home feeling sorry for herself? No! She overcame the expected depression that initially plagued her after the accident and has gone on to become a painter, author, workshop leader, evangelist, advocate for people with disabilities, nonprofit founder, and beloved wife.

Over 100,000 people around the world have received wheelchairs thanks to her organization, Wheels for the World. She has been appointed to national councils by two of our U.S. Presidents. In 2006, she published the *NLT Beyond Suffering Study Bible*, to encourage people in their times of suffering and those who care for them.[14]

Bill Gates's first business failed. Albert Einstein was mute until the age of four. Bethany Hamilton lost her arm to a shark. Benjamin Franklin dropped out of school at age ten. Sir Richard Branson suffered from dyslexia. Stephen King's first novel was rejected thirty times. Oprah Winfrey had a baby that died after she was molested by a family member when she was only fourteen. Van Gogh only sold one painting in his lifetime. Sylvester Stallone's face was partially paralyzed due to birth complications. Each of these challenges became fuel for success. This is more than mind over matter; it's the power of potential to do the impossible with God on your side.

LIMITLESS

Hollywood produced a movie in 2011 called *Limitless*. In the movie, there was a magic pill that, when taken, would allow a person to access one hundred percent of their brain power. By accessing the entirety of one's brain, the movie claimed, a person could live on an entirely new level, able to analyze, anticipate, focus, be more confident, and succeed in ways they never thought possible before tapping into this "enhanced" version of self. The movie appealed to millions of people who have believed the lie that we only use ten percent of our brains, and that if we could use a whopping fifteen percent, we would all be Einstein. The truth is, evidence shows that we actually do use one hundred percent of our brains every day.[15]

I have a hard time believing that is true of some teenagers, but let's press on . . .

According to the UCLA Brain Research Institute, the human brain has the ability and the potential to create, store. and learn virtually without limit. Their research indicates that we could, without any difficulty whatsoever, learn forty languages, memorize a set of encyclopedias from A to Z, and complete the required course work of twelve colleges and universities. Other studies show that your brain has the capacity to house as much information as the entire internet, and with far less impact on your electric bill.[16] That is your mental potential!

The English language has over a million words in it, more than any other language on the planet.[17] Yet linguistic experts estimate that our daily conversation uses up a mere 400 words, and the majority of those words are: me, my, mine, I, and why. Why, "why"? Because, for most of America's couch potatoes, it is too much work to obtain knowledge through study. Studying is to most Americans like going to the dentist for a root canal without any Novocain. Torture. Why do you think Google and Alexa are so popular? They do the work, so you don't have to.

What if we looked to the Bible for answers, instead of to Hollywood? In the pages of Scripture, you'll discover that you don't need a magic pill access your untapped potential. The power of potential is right there at your fingertips.

Paul said, "Study to shew thyself approved unto God, a workman that needeth not to be ashamed, rightly dividing the word of truth" (2 Timothy 2:15, KJV).

David said, "Thy word have I hid in mine heart, that I might not sin against thee" (Psalm 119:11, KJV). This could be translated, "I have read the Word until I've memorized it." Hiding something in your heart is memorization.

Just reading the Bible opens your mind to the power of this message. It increases your intellectual capacity to learn. Can you imagine if you read the Bible as much as you watched television? You'd be a genius! That's not puff talk; that's reality.

Solomon said,

Happy is the man who finds wisdom,
And the man who gains understanding;
For her proceeds are better than the profits of silver,
And her gain than fine gold.
She is more precious than rubies,
And all the things you may desire
    cannot compare with her.
Length of days is in her right hand,
In her left hand riches and honor.
Her ways are ways of pleasantness,
And all her paths are peace (Proverbs 3:13–17, NKJV).

Would you like a life that is better than silver and gold, more precious than rubies and diamonds, and led to pure peace? It is available to you. All you have to do is open your Bible.

KNOWLEDGE IS POWER

The first principle in releasing your potential is to gain the knowledge of God. The Bible is the fountain of knowledge. The author of that extraordinary text is God, the Holy Spirit. When you read the pages of Scripture, your life of doubt and insecurity will vanish. Your dull, dreary, dead personality will catch fire.

The Bible is a two-edged sword that will send you out to conquer.

Jesus is the Bread of Life who satisfies every longing, and the Living Water that makes every person totally satisfied.

The Bible has the answer to every crisis that you are facing or will ever face. I'd rather have one page out of the Bible than every book in the Harvard Library.

This book is the moral compass for America. And let me tell you, the moral compass of America is broken because we have not read and adhered to its principles! We need to turn off fake news and pick up the Good News. We, as a nation, are in a battle for the survival of our society.

Are we going to be a righteous nation under God, or a socialist nation under the dictates of the god called "socialism"? We can't be lukewarm any longer. I pray that God will spit the lukewarm out of His mouth! We need to commit to our future if we are going to change the course of American history.

It's impossible for America to fulfill her destiny with thirteen-year-olds having babies. It's impossible for America to serve as a shining city on a hill with fifteen-year-olds killing each other in the streets, or seventeen-year-olds dying of drug overdoses.

It's impossible for America to survive, much less thrive, with eighteen-year-olds getting a high school diploma that they can't even read. The mobs who pull down statues of George Washington and Frederick Douglas are a testimonial to the abject failure of the public education system of the United States of America.

What are we, as Christians, doing to call people to a higher standard, to point the next generation to their potential and purpose, which is so much greater than this?

It's time for us to rise. I'm tired of God's children saying, "I don't have much potential." You've heard the excuses: "I was born poor, my daddy was poor, my granddaddy was poor." Let me tell you: little is much when God is in it.

When God gets in your little bit, He'll make it a whole lot. He can turn your rowboat into the Queen Mary. In every seed, there's the potential of a harvest. In every bird, there's a flock. In every cow, there's a herd. In every fish, there's a school. In every man, there's a nation to be born Abraham had Isaac; Isaac produced Jacob; Jacob produced twelve sons, and those sons populated the righteous earth.

Pastors of the world, just because your church is small does not mean it cannot have great potential.

Bethlehem's manger was not the Marriott, but what happened there changed the course of the world. The stone that killed Goliath was small, but it changed the destiny of Israel. A mustard seed is very small, about the size of a bb, but the Lord says, "if you have faith as a mustard seed, you will say to this mountain, 'Move from here to there,' and it will move; and nothing will be impossible for you" (Matthew 17:20, NKJV). Even the tiniest bit of pure faith can move mountains.

God's mathematics works like this: one equals many; little equals much; small equals great; less equals more.

LEAVE THE PAST IN THE PAST

God never consults your past to determine your future. Your potential is not what you have done. That is your history, and there is no such thing as potential history. Your yesterdays are not nearly as important as your tomorrows.

Some destroy their potential by living in the glow of some shining moment in the past. If you are in sales, did you break all sales records last year? Forget it. You can starve to death remembering how great you used to be. Did your business have its finest year last year? Forget it. The economy could plummet this year, and you'll be looking for a job in the next twelve months. Students, did you make the honor roll last year? Forget it. Go home and do your homework and do it with excellence. The challenge is still in front of you. You didn't learn all there is to know. Athletes, did you make the all-star team last year? Forget it. That was last year. Turn off the TV, get off the couch, go exercise, lift weights, run and improve your athletic skills, or next year you could be sitting on the bench.

Your potential is in the business you can do but haven't done yet. Your potential is in the grades you can make but haven't made yet. Your potential is in the souls you can win but haven't won yet. If you've won a soul to Christ, win two. If you've won two, win four. If you've won four, win eight. If you've won eight, win sixteen and thirty-two and sixty-four. Let those multiples run because nothing is impossible with God.

Do you know how quickly America could turn around if we would just realize the power of multiplication? Reports claim there are sixty-two million evangelicals in America.[18] If every one of us won one soul to Christ each year, in four years we would dominate this country with the glory of God. That's a fact! But we've got to get Jesus out of the church buildings and into people's homes. The unchurched are suffering. They need to hear the Gospel message of faith, hope and love.

Are you tormented about your past? Out of the pages of Scripture pours: joy unspeakable and full of glory, peace in the midst of the storm, and the love of God that heals and unifies. Hope that is unshakeable and unbreakable can be found in the pages of Scripture. With the Lord as your Savior, your sin is made whiter than snow. Your past is buried in the deepest sea, never to be remembered against you anymore. The Bible says, "rejoice and be exceedingly glad" (Matthew 5:12, NKJV), because God Almighty is your Father and heaven is your home. You are a child of the King. Nothing shall be impossible unto you.

POWER SOURCE

When God creates something, He finds a special substance, a source, and creates out of that. As long as the created stays in contact with its source, its life has unlimited power and potential.

When God created plants, He chose dirt as the source. As long as plants stay in touch with dirt, they live. But pull a plant out of dirt, and it will die.

Fish were created for the water. Leave them there and they will become a school of fish. But a fish out of water will die.

When God created Adam, He took the dust of the ground and blew the breath of life into that clay temple. Adam and Eve, you and I, we all came from the breath of God. God is our Source. We are created in His image. So as long as you stay in contact with your Source, so long as you stay rooted and grounded in Him, your potential is limitless.

To those who came from Him, He imparts power: the power to lay hands on the sick so they shall recover, the power to command demon spirits to leave, power over the world, the flesh, and the devil, power over principalities, the power of His blood, the power of His Gospel, the power of His Kingdom.

If you are truly with the Lord and He is in you, His characteristics will be your characteristics. God is faithful. Are you? God is merciful. Are you? God gives unconditional love to people who don't deserve to be loved — people like you and me. Do you? God is totally forgiving. Are you? God is patient. Are you? Or do you find yourself standing in front of the microwave screaming, "Hurry up!"?

So long as you stay in contact with your Source, you can do great things. Abraham came out of an idolatrous society where the people fashioned gods out of wood and stone. The people could touch them. Yet Abraham had the faith to believe in an unseen, untouchable God. You too can feel supreme love for the One you've never seen. You can talk to God, whom you've never touched.

In God's economy, you empty yourself to become full. You decrease that you may increase. You go down in order to get up. You are strongest when you are weak. You are rich when you are poor. You give things away so that you can keep them forever. You die so that you can live forever. Let me tell you: death is not a tragedy; death is a reward! We're going to live forever! One day soon I will shake off these dry 80-year-old bones and dance free of pain, sickness, or disease into the sweet by and by!

With God as your Source: you see the invisible; you hear the inaudible; you know the unknowable, because you are sons and daughters of the Most-High God. All knowledge and all power flows through you because you are rooted and grounded in Him, rooted and grounded in the Word of God. He is the vine and we are the branches — the fruit will follow. Dare to believe that the impossible is possible for you when you stay connected to the Source!

BY FAITH

"And God said, Let us make man in our image, after our likeness . . ." (Genesis 1:26, KJV). The Hebrew word "likeness" means "to operate like," not "look like." If you're not functioning like God, you are malfunctioning. So the question is: How does God operate? God operates by faith. So, in order to be functioning properly, you must be operating in faith.

> . . . *without faith it is impossible to please*
> *God* . . . (Hebrews 11:6, NIV).

Faith is not an option; it's a requirement.

> . . . *the just shall live by faith* . . . (Hebrews 10:38, KJV).

Faith is not fiction; it's a fact.

> ... *And this is the victory that has overcome*
> *the world — our faith* (1 John 5:4, NKJV).

Faith does not demand miracles; faith creates miracles.

> *Now faith is the substance of things hoped for, the*
> *evidence of things not seen* (Hebrews 11:1, KJV).

Faith is not an emotion; it's something you can hold on to.

> *Who are kept by the power of God through*
> *faith unto salvation ready to be revealed*
> *in the last time* (1 Peter 1:5, KJV).

Faith is not a leap in the dark; it's a walk in the light.

> *We do not want you to become lazy, but to imitate*
> *those who through faith and patience inherit*
> *what has been promised* (Hebrews 6:12, NIV).

Faith is not hoping God is real; faith is knowing God is real, based on the evidence of the Word of God.

> *Then Jesus said to him, "Go your way; your faith has*
> *made you well." And immediately he received his sight*
> *and followed Jesus on the road* (Mark 10:52, NKJV).

God healed then, therefore He can heal now. God performed miracles then, so we know God can perform miracles now. God can move mountains. He can divide seas.

He can rain bread from heaven. If it's in the Bible, you can have it! "You have not because you ask not" (Luke 11:9).

NEVER UNDERESTIMATE A CHILD

Harvard social psychologist Robert Rosenthal gave a standard IQ test to all the children in one San Francisco grade school. Rosenthal told teachers that the test could predict which students had a high potential for improvement over the course of the school year. His researchers then drew random names out of a hat and told the teachers that these were the children who would excel. The teachers assumed that the children on the list had done well on the test and treated them accordingly. They treated the randomly chosen children on the list as if they were high achievers because they thought they were.

Rosenthal's theory proved correct: the students who were *expected* to improve did, averaging four improvement points higher than the students who the teachers were told not to expect improvement from. The highest rate of improvement was shown in the younger grades — first and second graders showing the most marked improvement. One student who had previously been labeled "mentally retarded" even went from an IQ of 61 to 106![19] Everyone can excel when someone believes in them, but most especially a child.

One day, a father was showing his son photographs of the most-wanted criminals in America on the post office wall. The father said, "These men are wanted all over this country. The police are looking for them. The FBI is looking for them. The CIA is looking for them." The child looked at the father and said, "Well, why didn't they keep those people when they took their pictures?" Not bad logic. Never underestimate a child!

One of the marks of socialism is to get the children away from the parents as soon as possible. Get them into schools where there is no Bible and there is no prayer and there is no right teaching. It has been said that Christianity is but one generation away from extinction.[20]

That's true. Children have been separated from the Word of God, but you can't blame the schools. If you send a hoodlum to school at eight o'clock, a hoodlum will come home at three-thirty. Your job as a parent is to teach them at home to read and pray, pray and obey.

Mrs. Susanna Wesley gave birth to nineteen children, and ten survived. She vowed to always spend more time with the Lord than she did at leisure; so, to get privacy, she would throw her apron over her head and pray and read Scripture for two hours every day. Her kids knew that when mama was under her "tent," she was only to be interrupted in a dire emergency.

Having been born into a family of twenty-five children, Susanna knew how rare and valuable one-on-one time was between a parent and a child. So, she not only home-schooled her children, teaching them to read and raising them with a Bible education, she also took the time, one-on-one, to pray with each child. Each child had their night of the week when they knew they would have that one-on-one time to pray with their mother. That upbringing was foundational to the founding of the Methodist church by two of her sons, John and Charles Wesley.[21]

Consider this: When God wanted to liberate Israel from Egypt's bondage, He sent a baby in a wicker basket. That child, who was named Moses, became a man of righteousness. When God wanted to liberate you and me from the debtor's prison of sin and Satan, He sent a baby in Bethlehem's manger named Jesus Christ. It is because of His sacrifice at the cross that we are called sons and daughters of the almighty, all-knowing God.

When God wanted to feed the multitudes, He packed it all into a little boy's sack lunch. When He wanted to heal Naaman of leprosy, He sent His message through a little servant girl. The Apostle Paul wrote to young Timothy, "Let no one despise your youth, but be an example to the believers in word, in conduct, in love, in spirit, in faith, in purity" (1 Timothy 4:12, NKJV). God believes in you the same way that Paul believed in Timothy and Susanna Wesley believed in each of her children.

Joel prophesied that old men would dream dreams, young men would see visions, and sons and daughters would prophesy (see Joel 2:28). There is no age limit on potential. At the age of almost 100 years, He and Sarah, age 90, produced the "son of laughter," named Isaac. It changed the course of the entire world. Isaac had twelve sons who produced the twelve tribes of Israel. Those twelve tribes produced the Old Testament prophets, King David, and thirty generations later, Jesus Christ. Whether you are a young visionary or an old dreamer, your potential is still limitless under the power of the almighty hand of God.

THE GREATEST TRAGEDY

Have you ever gone house hunting on a budget? Whenever you do anything on a budget, you know you are not looking for something perfect; you are looking for something "as is." As is, the roof may be caving in. As is, the windows may be broken. As is, the carpet may look and smell like it's from 1979. As is, the lawn may be missing in the weeds. As is, it may look like a disaster, but a person who can see potential will call that chaotic mess "good bones," and that hole in the roof "a perfect spot for a skylight." Broken windows are an opportunity for greater energy efficiency and the likelihood of solid-wood floors underneath that 70s carpet.

When God looks at you, He doesn't see a hopeless cause; He sees potential. He loves you "as is," but He loves you too much to leave you that way.

If God has given each of His children unlimited potential to do great things in this life, why isn't everyone living joy-filled, successful, abundant lives? There are two main things I see hindering people's potential: excuse making and instant gratification.

There are people who make good and there are people who make excuses.

Common excuses I've heard over the years:

"I'm too young." Well, Jesus started out as a baby in Bethlehem's manger, and, as a 13-year-old, was teaching Jewish theologians in the Temple. God Almighty used David to kill a giant when he was a teenager, and He used a teenage girl named Mary to give birth to the Son of God in a manger.

"I'm too old." Moses was eighty when he got his start in the ministry that crushed the Egyptian empire.

"I'm not talented enough." A mustard seed isn't much, but if it can grow the tallest tree then your little bit is plenty! Little is much when God is in it. Jesus fed 5000 with a boy's sack lunch.

"I don't know the right people." You know God the Father, God the Son, and God the Holy Spirit; you are well connected to receive supernatural power. (Acts 1:8)

"I don't have enough education." Eliza was sixteen when she married twenty-year-old Andrew. Andrew was a tailor who had never been to school. He couldn't read, write, or spell. But Eliza believed in her husband and she taught him how to read. Her husband, Andrew Johnson, later became our seventeenth president.[22]

Do you think it's important for a songwriter to be able to read music? Have you ever heard the songs "White Christmas," "God Bless America," or "Cheek to Cheek"? They were composed by Irving Berlin, a singing waiter in Chinatown, who couldn't read music. And George Gershwin called Irving Berlin "the greatest songwriter who has ever lived."[23]

When some blank canvases that American artist James Whistler ordered got lost in the mail, he was asked if they were of any value, to which he replied, "Not yet, not yet."[24] That's potential!

Stop whining. Stop making excuses. Take charge of your life. Believe in the power of your potential. When you blame someone else for your inability to do something, you have empowered that person to control you. They are now in charge of your life. Take charge of your life or someone else will! No more excuses!

The second way people destroy their potential is by demanding instant gratification. They want microwave Christianity. They want love without commitment. They want benefits without responsibility. They want success without work. Well, the only place you're going to find success before work is in the dictionary!

Winston Churchill said, "Continuous effort — not strength or intelligence — is the key to unlocking our potential."[25] The goal is not to be an overnight success, or to be in the right place at the right time. The goal is hard work, never giving up, and learning to be patient with the process.

The story goes that a man was pushing a shopping cart around a supermarket when his baby started wailing and crying uncontrollably. As the man pushed the cart up and down the aisles he kept repeating in a soothing voice, "Keep calm, George. Don't get excited, George. Relax, George. There's no need to yell, George." A lady watching, who had more than once been in the same situation when her own children were young, said encouragingly, "You are certainly to be commended for your patience in trying to quiet little George." "Lady," he said, "I'm George!"[26]

I remind parents of children that someday those kids of yours will grow up, and if you've done anything right, they'll move out. But parents have to be patient with the process. After a few more years, when your children are about thirty-five or forty-years-old, they will come back and say, "You were right about everything. You were right." That doesn't come easy and it doesn't come quick, but the Apostle Paul tells us to press on with the end goal in mind and one day you will receive the prize.

Refuse to make excuses. Add to your life: patience, persistence, hard work, staying connected to the Source and study of the Word. You'll soon discover a potential that is endless, limitless, exponential, infinite, and upward!

The greatest tragedy in life is not death. The greatest tragedy in life is to fail to fulfill your purpose and potential. The fact that you were born is proof that God has an assignment for you. God has something special planned for every believer. Don't you dare go to your grave with unused God-given talent, with unfulfilled God-inspired dreams, and with missed God-ordained opportunities.

Physicists tell us that the hydrogen contained in a glass of water holds the atomic fusion potential to power a battleship around the world four times. Likewise, there is enormous power in your untapped potential.

Don't bury your talent! Invest in your potential. Put your talent to work. Release the power of God that is within you and reach for greatness! And one day, when the trumpet of God sounds for you and an angelic escort carries you up to meet Jesus in the sky, God the Father will have these words for you: ". . . 'Well done, good and faithful servant! . . . Come and share your master's happiness!'" (Matthew 25:21, NIV).

Know for certain that it is the Lord's will for every believer to walk in the authority that His Word affords. As you learn to release the Absolute power of His Word, you'll will soon experience God's supernatural peace, unconditional joy and abundant success in every area of your life.

THREE

THE POWER OF FORGIVENESS

"Forgetting is something that time alone takes care of, but forgiveness is an act of volition, and only the sufferer is qualified to make the decision." -SIMON WIESENTHAL[27]

"To forgive is to set a prisoner free and discover that the prisoner was you." -LEWIS SMEDES[28]

On February 9, 1960, Adolph Coors III, grandson of Adolph Coors, the founder of Coors Brewing Company, disappeared after stopping on the side of the road to help what appeared to be a stranded motorist. A nationwide manhunt ensued, the largest FBI effort since the Lindbergh baby kidnapping. Joseph Corbett, Jr., an escaped prisoner, was later arrested and charged with the crime — a kidnapping gone wrong that ended in murder. Coors's clothing, monogrammed pocketknife, and skull were discovered seven months later in a garbage dump on a remote mountainside in Colorado.[29]

The Coors family was no stranger to tragedy. The first Adolph Coors died by suicide when he stepped out a sixth story hotel window. A kidnapping plot against the second Coors was discovered just in time. Later, the wife of Adolph Coors III died tragically when she fell down a flight of stairs at a friend's house. That's enough to harden anyone's heart.

Adolph Coors III left behind four children, including his fourteen-year-old son, Adolph Coors IV, who turned fifteen three days after his father's remains were found. The younger Coors remembers going to church with his siblings, praying that their father would be found alive. When that didn't turn out to be the case, he abandoned God and spent years struggling. He went off on his own, then returned to the Coors Brewing Plant where his uncle let him work as a tour guide — Adolph Coors IV and his siblings were no longer heirs to the Coors empire after their father's body had been found. He went off on his own again, then came back to the plant once more. This time his uncle put him in charge of cleaning the vats.

It was around that time that Adolph Coors IV and his wife entertained a Christian couple in their home. They realized they wanted what the Christian couple had, and both were led to accept Jesus as their Lord and Savior. Coors reflects on his time cleaning vats at the brewing company as a time when he felt closest to God — all that time scrubbing and praying did a wonder on his life and his heart.

Later a friend asked Coors if he had forgiven his father's killer. Coors said yes, but the friend told him that the deepest forgiveness happens face-to-face.

Coors initially felt angry at his friend. How dare he tell Coors he needed to sit down face-to-face with the man who had stolen everything from him! Coors realized there was still anger and resentment in his heart. The hatred was eating him on the inside. Rage and resentment simmered beneath the surface of his life. Coors realized that his friend was right, and he needed to not only forgive but seek forgiveness from the man who had murdered his father.

Through the power of the Holy Spirit, Adolph Coors IV visited the maximum-security unit of Colorado's Cañon City Penitentiary. He asked to see Joseph Corbett,

Jr., but Corbett refused to see him. Coors expected to feel relief, but instead he felt sorrow and disappointment that could only be explained by God's presence in his life. Coors asked if he could leave something for the prisoner. He left a Bible, with a note tucked inside. On the note, he had written:

I'm here today to ask for your forgiveness for the hatred I've had in my heart for you. I forgive you for what you've done to my family. I hope someday to sit down with you and share with you the joy I have found in Christ.

Coors's faith had taught him that he was no less guilty than Corbett. Jesus said that there is no difference between physically killing and killing in your heart. While Corbett had taken the physical life of his father, Coors had murdered his father's killer over and over in his heart. We are all sinners who fall short of the glory of God. We all stand in need of mercy and forgiveness. Coors came to the powerful, liberating realization that he not only needed to forgive, but be forgiven. He went away from that penitentiary with a peace that surpasses all understanding and a love for that man that could only have been put in his heart by Jesus Christ. That is power. That is the power of forgiveness.[30]

Jesus proclaimed in Matthew 5,

"Therefore if you bring your gift to the altar, and there remember that your brother has something against you, leave your gift there before the altar, and go your way. First be reconciled to your brother, and then come and offer your gift." (Matthew 5:23–24, NKJV)

Here Jesus establishes what I call the "you make the first move" principle of relational restoration. It's not enough to whisper forgiveness into the dark. It's not enough to *think* forgiveness. Jesus exhorts us to go to that person and be reconciled. Whatever it is — a grudge, resentment, anger, bitterness, a history of abuse — you must make the first move toward reconciliation.

"Stop praying," Jesus said, because God cannot hear you over the hardness in your heart.

Make a phone call. Send a letter. Show up on their doorstep or their prison cell. Make the first move to remove the barriers of resentment that exist between you and another person. If they reject your efforts, that's on them. You won't be judged by their response, but by your actions. After you have made the effort toward reconciliation, you are clear to return to the altar to be heard of God with a clear conscience and a clean heart.

FORGIVENESS IS NOT OPTIONAL

Forgive me for being so blunt, but if you don't practice forgiveness, it will destroy the quality of your life on earth and even put at risk your entry through the gates of heaven.

Write that on your bathroom mirror. Forgiveness is that important.

These words in Scripture are written in red because they are the words that Jesus spoke:

"For if you forgive men their trespasses, your heavenly Father will also forgive you. But if you do not forgive men their trespasses, neither will your Father forgive your trespasses." (Matthew 6:14–15, NKJV)

Forgiveness is serious business, but it isn't complicated. You don't need a seminary degree to understand that when you forgive, you will be forgiven; and when you don't forgive, God will not forgive you.

The Lord's Prayer endorses heaven's policy on forgiveness: "And forgive us our debts, as we forgive our debtors" (Matthew 6:12, KJV). We recite that prayer but seldom practice it. It's not only important to know the words but understand its message and obey it. Forgiveness is not optional. If the Bible teaches anything, it teaches *that*. The Word and the will of God are made perfectly clear: We can freely ask God's forgiveness once we have fully forgiven others.

Saint Paul wrote, "And be ye kind one to another, tenderhearted, forgiving one another, even as God for Christ's sake hath forgiven you" (Ephesians 4:32, KJV). When I was a boy, my mother made my older brother Bill and me quote that verse to each other every time we got in a ruckus, which was about three times a week.

I had that verse memorized before almost any other. It still rolls off my tongue with ease: "And be ye kind one to another, tenderhearted, forgiving one another, even as God for Christ's sake hath forgiven you." But the fact that my brother and I said it so much was an indication that we knew the words, but we weren't getting the message. Get the message!

Paul continued teaching the New Testament Church by saying,

> Therefore, as the elect of God, holy and beloved, put on tender mercies, kindness, humility, meekness, longsuffering; bearing with one another, and forgiving one another, if anyone has a complaint against another; even as Christ forgave you, so you also must do. (Colossians 3:12–13, NKJV)

This truth is clearly affirmed by God, Jesus, and Paul — forgiveness is not optional! If you won't forgive another person, God will not forgive you. The words "forgive" and "forgiveness" appear sixty-six times in the New Testament, and one-third of those are tied to the forgiveness of others.[31] Why so many? Because the power of forgiveness is that important.

THE EXAMPLE OF JESUS

While painting *The Last Supper*, Leonardo da Vinci purportedly painted the face of his own mortal enemy on Judas, the man who betrayed Jesus to his death. But then da Vinci suddenly came up with the painter's equivalent of writer's block. He only had one face to finish, but he couldn't go on. It wasn't until he wiped the face of Judas clean that he was able to complete the final face — the face of Jesus.[32]

It was during that Last Supper with his disciples that Jesus announced that one of them, who was dipping his bread in the same dish that Jesus used, would betray him. All of the disciples denied that they would do any such thing. Even Judas said, "Surely it is not I, Rabbi?", to which Jesus replied, "You have said it yourself" (Matthew 26:25, NASB).

Judas went on his way and Jesus went to the Mount of Olives to pray. He knew what was coming, and He knew who would betray Him. Yet, when Judas showed up with a loud, angry mob, Jesus said to His disciple, "Friend, do what you have come for" (Matthew 26:50, NASB). Even in the moment of being betrayed, Jesus calls His betrayer "friend"!

But that is not even the greatest act of forgiveness that Jesus did in His lifetime. In His final moments, having been beaten and torn and ridiculed and hung on a cross to die, Jesus demonstrated the act of forgiveness that we, as Christian believers, are to follow. His exact words on the cross were: "Father, forgive them; for they know not what they do" (Luke 23:34, KJV).

Our Redeemer used His last breath to forgive a brutal Roman empire that had harassed Him and His family from the day of His birth. As blood flowed from His hands and feet, mercy flowed from His lips. They killed Him because they feared Him. They feared Him because He healed, He raised the dead, He used a boy's sack lunch to feed a multitude, and He upset their sense of order. They didn't kill Him because they thought He was the Prince of Peace. They killed Him because He was considered an insurrectionist too dangerous to be allowed to live. Jesus was crucified because He fought a battle for your soul and mine. On that cross He shed his blood for the forgiveness of sin — my sin, your sin, the iniquity of the whole world's sin — forgiven and forgotten, buried in the deepest sea, never to be remembered any more.

NEW BEGINNINGS

Three days after the crucifixion, when the women went to the tomb to anoint Jesus's body with special oils, they found an angel instead of a body. The angel said to them, "But go, tell His disciples — and Peter — that He is going before you into Galilee; there you will see Him, as He said to you" (Mark 16:7, NKJV). Tell His disciples — *and Peter*. Why the emphasis on Peter? Because prior to the crucifixion, Peter denied Jesus three times.

Peter, who liked to make grandiose statements that he couldn't back up, said to Jesus in the Upper Room, "Even if everyone else deserts you, I will never desert you" (Matthew 26:33, NLT). Peter then falls asleep while he's supposed to be praying for Jesus, reacts impulsively cutting off Malchus's ear, and then denies Jesus three times. Well done, Peter.

Let's take a quick look at those denials. First, Peter lied to a servant girl who asked if he'd been with Jesus: "I don't know what you're talking about." Then he lied to another servant girl who said he most definitely had been with Jesus: "I don't even know the man!" Finally, he lied to a group of bystanders who recognized his accent as Galilean: "I DON'T KNOW HIM!" (see Luke 22:54–62).

Peter is oblivious to his betrayal until a crowing rooster reminds Him of the Master's prophecy. The sound triggers a flood of remembrance and understanding. He had vowed to go to jail or even to death for Jesus. Peter wept bitterly in shame and regret: *What would Jesus, his Messiah and friend, think of him now?*

Thus, it is no accident that the angel encourages Mary Magdalene to tell the disciples *and Peter* to meet Jesus in Galilee. Galilee! It was on the shores of that vast lake that Jesus had first called Peter and his brother Andrew to follow him. And there, the risen Jesus would instruct Peter to cast his net on the other side (see John 21). When Peter realized it was Jesus, he jumped ship and headed straight for his risen Lord. In that poignant reunion Jesus forgave Peter by giving the fisherman the opportunity to declare his love for Him three times — one for each denial.

Forgiveness is a full pardon. It's a fresh start. It's another chance. It's a new beginning. It's a lifting of a heavy burden and the canceling of a debt.

After twenty-seven years in prison, when Nelson Mandela became president of South Africa, he invited one of his white wardens to the inauguration.[33]

After her husband, Jim, was murdered by a tribal people in Ecuador, Elisabeth Elliot and her young daughter went to live with the tribe. This act of forgiveness allowed Elisabeth to lead many of those tribal members to Christ.[34]

After Charles Roberts, a milk truck driver, killed five children and then himself in the Amish community of West Nickel Mines, Pennsylvania, the community, including the parents of the murdered children, showed up for the funeral of Charles Roberts, hugging his bereaved widow and donating money to help her and her children in the aftermath. This act of forgiveness inspired a nation and freed the Nickel Mines community to grieve without the burden of unforgiveness in their hearts.[35]

Where does this power to forgive come from? It comes from God, through the power of the Holy Spirit, and through the witness of our Lord and Savior Jesus Christ. Jesus forgave Peter, the rock upon which His church would be built, and gave him a fresh start, including the keys to the kingdom:

> *"And I tell you, you are Peter, and on this rock I will build my church, and the gates of hell shall not prevail against it. I will give you the keys of the kingdom of heaven, and whatever you bind on earth shall be bound in heaven, and whatever you loose on earth shall be loosed in heaven."* (Matthew 16:18–19, ESV)

Paul wrote,

> *If you forgive anyone, I also forgive him. And if I have forgiven anything, I have forgiven it in the presence of Christ for your sake, in order that Satan should not outwit us. For we are not unaware of his schemes.* (2 Corinthians 2:10–11, BSB)

The devil will try to trick you with his schemes, his devices, his sly ways. One of those strategies is to try to trap you in unforgiveness, which will completely destroy the quality of your life and steal the peace in your heart. Don't give him an opening. Slam the door in the devil's face. Forgive, and move on to new beginnings.

THE DEMANDS OF FORGIVENESS

The forgiveness that Jesus taught is not soft-hearted, mush-mouthed foolishness. Forgiveness is full of compassion, but it demands a change in conduct. Hear this: to forgive another person without demanding a change in their conduct is to make the grace of God an accomplice to evil. That may be the most powerful statement you have ever read, so read it again: *To forgive another person without demanding a change in their conduct is to make the grace of God an accomplice to evil.*

Look at this story told of a woman caught in adultery:

Then the scribes and Pharisees brought to Him a woman caught in adultery. And when they had set her in the midst, they said to Him, "Teacher, this woman was caught in adultery, in the very act. Now Moses, in the law, commanded us that such should be stoned. But what do You say?" (John 8:3–5, NKJV)

The Pharisees were always trying to trap Jesus. Whether it was putting a blind man on His path so that they could accuse Him of working on the Sabbath or attempting to outwit Him with their vast knowledge of Mosaic law, they focused all their energy and attention on trying to make Jesus look bad. Imagine if they had spent half that time and energy learning from Him what they could have accomplished for the kingdom!

This they said, testing Him, that they might have something of which to accuse Him. But Jesus stooped down and wrote on the ground with His finger, as though He did not hear. (v. 6, NKJV)

If you've ever stuck your fingers in your ears and said, "I can't hear you!", you know how aggravating this can be to your questioner. Jesus refused to engage or even acknowledge the Pharisees. You can just imagine the sound of their blood boiling as each second passed by in silence.

So when they continued asking Him, He raised Himself up and said to them, "He who is without sin among you, let him throw a stone at her first." And again He stooped down and wrote on the ground. Then those who heard it, being convicted by their conscience, went out one by one, beginning with the

*oldest even to the last. And Jesus was left alone, and
the woman standing in the midst.* (vv. 7–9, NKJV)

Jesus's silence didn't shut them up, but He knew
what would. You've no doubt heard the saying, 'when you
point your finger at someone, you have three more pointing back at you.' This is precisely the argument that Jesus
used on the Pharisees. If those fingers pointing back at
you come up clean, free from sin, then go ahead. Find the
biggest rock you can lift and throw it at her. In fact, be
the *first* to throw rocks at her to prove just how right and
pure and without sin you are.

*When Jesus had raised Himself up and saw no
one but the woman, He said to her, "Woman,
where are those accusers of yours? Has no
one condemned you?"* (v. 10, NKJV)

The Pharisees may have had impure motives. Their
method may have been all wrong. But they weren't
about to claim personal perfection. The oldest and wisest among the bunch were the first to drop their stones,
tuck tail, and leave. They were followed one-by-one by
those with the pride that comes with youth, until only
Jesus was left to judge the woman.

She said, "No one, Lord." And Jesus said to her, "Neither do I condemn you; go and sin no more." (v. 11, NKJV)

Jesus had every right to judge the woman. He alone was without sin, perfect in every way. Yet He refused to condemn her. He forgave her, but forgiveness did not come without its own demand: "go and sin no more." His point was clear: *"I forgive you, but I expect you to change your conduct."*

It is true that God will forgive you of all sin that is confessed and forsaken, but you can't just do the confessing without the forsaking.

Traditional wedding vows ask the bride and groom to take one another "for better or worse, for richer or poorer, in sickness and health, and forsaking all others." You can't marry and keep one of those vows but ignore all the others. You must give up your life as a playboy if you want the blessings that come from a godly marriage.

This principle is found in the wisdom of Solomon, in Proverbs 28:13, which says, "He who covers his sins will not prosper, but whoever confesses and forsakes them will have mercy" (NKJV). If you don't forsake your sin — which means to renounce, to turn away from, to give it up — then you're in trouble and not walking in the grace and mercy of the Lord. Simply stated, when God forgives you of sin, He expects you to stop it. Period. Go and sin no more!

THREE-STEP PROCESS

Christ not only forgave us our sins, but He also taught us a powerful three-step pattern so that we too could extend forgiveness.

Step One: Forgive Immediately. Remember in Matthew 5:23–24 when Jesus says that if you are praying and remember that you have something against another, what are you to do? Drop the sacrifice and go. Go! Go immediately because God can't hear you over your façade. Go and forgive and receive forgiveness. Forgive immediately.

Step Two: Be Reconciled. In that same passage, Jesus says, "be reconciled" (v. 24). Go and make it right. Do what you can to resolve the issue and be reunited with your brethren. Remember that when Adolph Coors IV went to prison to meet with his father's killer, the man would not meet with him. You can't control another person's response. Coors couldn't control that, but what he could control was his part. He forgave and he went to be reconciled. God honored his action by bestowing upon him a peaceful heart, and God will do the same for you.

Step Three: Forgive Totally. When you bury the hatchet, don't leave the handle sticking up out of the ground so you can take hold of the grudge once. Bury it, handle and all — once and for all.

Forgive immediately. Be reconciled. Forgive totally. That is the three-step pathway to unleashing the power to forgiveness.

SEVENTY TIMES SEVEN

In Matthew, chapter 18, Jesus has this powerful interaction with Peter:

> *Then Peter came to Him and said, "Lord, how often shall my brother sin against me, and I forgive him? Up to seven times?" Jesus said to him, "I do not say to you, up to seven times, but up to seventy times seven." (Matthew 18:21–22, NKJV)*

"Seven times," "seventy times seven," the message was clear: forgive, and keep on forgiving. Forgive totally, so that each act of forgiveness is like the first time.

To further illustrate his point, Jesus tells this story of the unmerciful slave:

> *"Therefore the kingdom of heaven is like a certain king who wanted to settle accounts with his servants. And when he had begun to settle accounts, one was brought to him who owed him ten thousand talents.*

But as he was not able to pay, his master commanded that he be sold, with his wife and children and all that he had, and that payment be made. The servant therefore fell down before him, saying, 'Master, have patience with me, and I will pay you all.' Then the master of that servant was moved with compassion, released him, and forgave him the debt.

"*But that servant went out and found one of his fellow servants who owed him a hundred denarii; and he laid hands on him and took him by the throat, saying, 'Pay me what you owe!' So his fellow servant fell down at his feet and begged him, saying, 'Have patience with me, and I will pay you all.' And he would not, but went and threw him into prison till he should pay the debt.*

"*So when his fellow servants saw what had been done, they were very grieved, and came and told their master all that had been done. Then his master, after he had called him, said to him, 'You wicked servant! I forgave you all that debt because you begged me. Should you not also have had compassion on your fellow servant, just as I had pity on you?' And his master was angry, and delivered him to the torturers until he should pay all that was due to him.*" (Matthew 18:23–34, NKJV)

Here we have a king who is trying to settle his accounts. And the king has a servant, a slave, who owes him a ton of money — millions of dollars, thousands of bags of gold. The king threatens to send the slave to prison, and his family too, but the slave asked for more time to pay off his debts.

The king took pity on the servant. In fact, the king took mercy to the next level. Instead of agreeing to let the servant work off his debt, the king wiped the slate clean, absolving the debt completely. Wow! Bang! The servant went from being millions in the hole to being debt-free with one fell swoop.

Now how do you think the servant decided to celebrate? The forgiven servant found a guy who owed him a fraction of what he'd owed the king — a few bags of silver, a thousand bucks; it might as well have been twenty dollars compared to the debt the servant had just been forgiven. But instead of forgiving the man's paltry debt, he throttled the guy, choking him right there on the street in front of everyone.

The coworker asked for the same opportunity that the servant had asked of the king: for patience, and time to repay the debt. But instead of showing the compassion which had been shown him, the servant had his coworker thrown into prison.

But justice would be served. The king got word of what had happened and sentenced the servant to a life of torment. End of story. Well, almost. Jesus adds one more note to his listeners: "So My heavenly Father also will do to you if each of you, from his heart, does not forgive his brother his trespasses" (Matthew 18:35, NKJV).

My friend, your knees better be knocking right about now, because that message wasn't just for then, it's also for now. For you and me. This is a twenty-first century message, and it doesn't get much clearer: when you will not forgive, you insist on subjecting yourself to tormentors. Who are the tormentors?

Medical science has labeled those "tormentors" as high blood pressure, ulcers, sleeplessness, depression, anger, and resentment. When you will not forgive, it will eat you alive. It will destroy the quality of your life, because forgiveness is essential to your eternal soul. It is essential for your mental health. It is essential for your physical healing. It is God's greatest gift to every person who has ever drawn a breath. Jesus paid the price, not only for you to be forgiven, but to give you the power of His Holy Spirit to forgive others.

PRODIGAL SON

The story is told of a rebellious young man who broke the law. He was sent to prison for eight long years. He knew his father was greatly disappointed in him, and that, after his release, his father probably wouldn't allow him to come back home. As the time of his release drew near, the young man sent his mother a letter. He told her that he was being released and that he would like to take the train home. He knew the route well.

The train would go up a steep hill and then along the side of their farm. He concluded the letter by writing, "If you and dad will let me come home again, please tie a piece of cloth in the oak tree beside the railroad track. If I see the ribbon of cloth, I'll get off the train. But if I don't see a ribbon, I'll just keep going and will know not to contact you ever again."

Well, the day of his release came. He walked out the prison gates and headed straight for the train station. He bought a ticket and boarded the next train. With every turn of the wheels, the tension mounted within him. Would there be a cloth of ribbon in that tree?

As the train rounded a bend and began the uphill climb that would lead to his family's farm, he couldn't stand to look. Fearing he would be rejected and unforgiven, he asked the young man sitting next to him, "Would you please look out the window and tell me if you see a ribbon of cloth tied in an old oak tree?"

The passenger looked out the window and said, "No, I don't see one ribbon. I see hundreds of ribbons tied to every branch in that tree. There are ribbons tied to the fence, the clothesline, the back porch. There are so many ribbons on that farm, it looks like it snowed! What does it mean?"

"It means I'm forgiven and I'm going back home," the young man said, as he hurried to gather his belongings and to disembark the train.

In Luke, chapter 15, Jesus tells the story of the prodigal son who squandered his inheritance while his father was still alive. Just like the young man in the story above, the prodigal son eventually returned home in rags, covered with the stench of swine, prepared to beg his father's forgiveness. Neither son expected the reception that waited for them.

The young man was met with a blizzard of ribbons, and the prodigal son in the Bible was met with a father who ran to him, embraced him, prepared a feast for him, and quickly forgave his wandering ways. The father said of the prodigal, "'For this my son was dead, and is alive again; he was lost, and is found.' And they began to celebrate" (Luke 15:24, ESV).

Just as the fathers in these two stories forgave their sons, God through Christ has forgiven us. And we are to go and do likewise. Jesus, our example, has given us the greatest gift. Don't squander it. Forgiveness can move you from death to life, from lost to found. The quality of your life depends on one word: forgiveness.

With all the above in mind, please let me ask you a few vital questions. If your life lacks peace, who do you need to forgive? If you are depressed, who do you need to forgive? If you are angry all the time and your spouse and kids don't even want to be around you, who do you need to forgive?

Forgiveness is the key that unlocks the prison door of hatred and resentment. Forgiveness is the power that breaks the chains of bitterness and anger. Forgiveness brings restoration and unity in your marriage, your family, and the Body of Christ. That is the power of forgiveness.

THE GREATEST FORGIVENESS STORY I'VE EVER HEARD

Let me conclude with the greatest forgiveness story I have ever heard. In the early 1970s, at an author's luncheon in Dallas, Texas, I had an encounter that was like God Almighty reaching down and kissing me on the forehead. I was seated at a table when a gracious, gray-haired lady sat next to me and, in the most loving voice, introduced herself as Corrie ten Boom.

Corrie ten Boom was a Dutch watchmaker who worked with her father, Casper, and sister, Betsie, to help the Jews escape the horror of the Holocaust during WWII. Corrie and her family hid the Jewish people in their home, in a secret room built into Corrie's bedroom wall, which led to the title of Corrie's blockbuster book, *The Hiding Place.*

Unfortunately, the ten Booms were caught, arrested by the Gestapo, and sent to a concentration camp. Casper ten Boom died shortly after their arrival. Corrie and Betsie and all the others were starved, beaten, and dehumanized. But the young women managed to smuggle a Bible into their camp. Their bunks were riddled with fleas, which kept the guards away and allowed them to read the Scriptures to one another, building their faith even as their bodies broke down. Eventually Betsie died in the camp. But Corrie managed to be released by some sort of clerical error that can only be explained by a miracle of God.

Years after the war ended, Corrie ten Boom met her most vicious Nazi captor face-to-face, a man who had mocked the women as they stood naked and shivering in the delousing showers. He was at a church where Corrie spoke about her experience and God's forgiveness. He came up to her afterwards and told her he was now a Christian, who had been forgiven by God. He extended his hand to her and asked for her forgiveness as well. Corrie prayed for God to give her the strength, and the feeling of total forgiveness. She raised her hand to meet his:

"And as I did, an incredible thing took place. The current started in my shoulder, raced down my arm, sprang into our joined hands. And then this healing warmth seemed to flood my whole being, bringing tears to my eyes.

'I forgive you, brother!' I cried. 'With all my heart.'

For a long moment we grasped each other's hands, the former guard and the former prisoner. I had never known God's love so intensely, as I did then. But even so, I realized it was not my love. I had tried, and did not have the power. It was the power of the Holy Spirit as recorded in Romans 5:5, '. . . because the love of God is shed abroad in our hearts by the Holy Ghost which is given unto us.'"[36]

Miss Corrie's reflection was similar to that of Adolph Coors IV. Both attributed their ability to forgive as an act of God and the power of the Holy Spirit, resulting in a peace that is beyond human comprehension.

Who are you holding prisoner through past offenses? Who is it that you refuse to forgive? If you want to have any kind of victorious life at all, you must absolutely forgive that person. Now that doesn't mean you have to be best friends afterward. But you do have to bury the hatchet without the handle sticking up. Don't even try to do it in your own strength. Pray for the strength, the power, the ability to extend your hand and forgive.

Remember this truth: God gives you the power to forgive, and to forgive is to set a prisoner free, and you will discover that the prisoner set free . . . was you.

THE POWER TO GET WEALTH

"God does not get wealth for you . . . God empowers you to get wealth." -PAUL DE JONG[37]

"I believe the power to make money is a gift from God. It is to be developed and used to the best of our ability, for the good of mankind. Having been endowed with the gift I possess, I believe it is my duty to make money and still more money, and to use the money I make for the good of my fellow man according to the dictates of my conscience." -JOHN D. ROCKEFELLER[38]

As a preacher of the Gospel, I've always tried to keep in mind a piece of wisdom from Sir Winston Churchill: "If you have an important point to make, don't try to be subtle or clever. Use a pile driver. Hit the point once. Then come back and hit it again. Then hit it a third time."[39]

So here's the pile driver question with a point: *When it comes to wealth, what do you want for your life?*

Many decades in ministry have led me to understand that financial freedom is something that almost everyone is looking for, but very few ever achieve. That's largely because every achievement in life demands a specific goal. Living life without a goal is like taking a vacation without a map. You might have some fun adventures, but you'll never reach your goal or experience the joy of success.

So what, specifically, do you want to achieve financially? When in your lifetime will you be able to say, "This is it. This is enough. I've reached my goal!"

It's possible that you simply want to make sure you will make enough money to educate your children. You have a specific retirement age in mind. You may be thinking about the end of your life, and what you want to leave behind for your spouse and children and grandchildren. You may want to pay off your credit cards and get off the treadmill of perpetual debt. (I often recommend plastic surgery as the quickest way to get out of credit card debt: cut up your credit cards and throw them in the trash!)

Whatever your goal, what I hope to show you in this chapter is that *you* have the power to get wealth that is sufficient to achieve financial freedom. The greatest financial manuscript in the world records: "And you shall remember the LORD your God, for it is He who gives you power to get wealth . . ." (Deuteronomy 8:18, NKJV).

Let's begin with a little orientation, remedial instruction, and perspective.

CONCERNING WEALTH MANAGEMENT

Here in the twenty-first century, it seems we live in a world in which everyone needs a refresher course on the basics of wealth management. Where can a person turn to find sound financial guidance for his future and the well-being of those he loves? Clearly, not the government! With the national debt nearing twenty-five trillion dollars as I write, it would take almost seventy years paying one million dollars A DAY just to break-even if our government stopped spending today.

A politician was walking down Pennsylvania Avenue in Washington D.C. when a thief leaped out of the shadows with a gun. "Give me your money or I'll blow your brains out!" he shouted. The politician calmly responded, "Go ahead and shoot. I've been in Washington D.C. for forty years. I know for a fact you can live here forever without brains but not five minutes without money."

You can seldom get sound financial advice from relatives or friends either. According to the Social Security Administration, only two percent of Americans reach age sixty-five financially independent. Thirty percent depend on charity, twenty-three percent must continue to work to survive, and forty-five percent are dependent on relatives.

According to Devaney's Economic Tables, fewer men have a net worth of one-hundred dollars at age sixty-five than at age eighteen. Think about it! After fifty years of work, they have less than two dollars per year to show for their efforts.

Something is seriously wrong with our economic policy. The problem is that we have ignored God's principles of prosperity and as a nation are saturated with debt and staring bankruptcy in the face. Welfare rolls are exploding, and socialists are being elected to the U.S. Congress and we the people are being suckered into paying for endless pipe dreams. The power to get wealth is a much-needed topic.

After more than sixty years in ministry and having accumulated three university degrees and three honorary doctorates, I can enthusiastically recommend the most astute financial guide ever printed: The Bible! The principles of finance and wealth management written by the Hand of God, the Holy Spirit, are absolutely infallible.

When Jesus of Nazareth was on the earth, He often used illustrations in His teachings to portray the power to get wealth. It is a fact that sixteen out of His thirty-eight parables taught His listeners on how to handle their finances. In the Bible, five times more is said about money management than is said about prayer. There are five-hundred verses on prayer and faith combined, yet over two-thousand verses dealing with how to master your money.

Jesus Christ, the Architect of the human soul, knew that men were attracted to the topic of wealth. Notice the themes of Jesus's parables in Matthew, chapter thirteen: "the kingdom of heaven is like treasure hidden in a field" (v. 44, NKJV), and "the kingdom of heaven is like a merchant seeking beautiful pearls, who, when he had found one pearl of great price, went and sold all that he had and bought it" (vv. 45–46, NKJV). Jesus knew exactly how to capture the attention of His audience and keep it.

With all that in view, I want to introduce you to ten financial principles from the Bible that will bring to you, and those you love, the power to get wealth. The first two of these correct two very common misconceptions.

PRINCIPLE ONE: GOD DELIGHTS IN YOUR PROSPERITY

Many believers have been told that God wants them poor. They've been assured that following Jesus involves a vow of poverty.

In contrast, the greatest manual ever written on the power to get wealth reads: "Beloved, I wish above all things that thou mayest prosper and be in health, even as thy soul prospereth" (3 John 1:2, KJV).

It continues: "This Book of the Law shall not depart from your mouth, but you shall meditate in it day and night, that you may observe to do according to all that is written in it. For then you will make your way prosperous, and then you will have good success" (Joshua 1:8, NKJV).

Note that the Lord tells Joshua to meditate "in" not "on" God's instructions. This is not some osmosis trick where you lay your head on the Holy Book at night and wake up with Bible bedhead and a fistful of fifty-dollar bills. No, you read the Bible, study the Bible, talk about the Bible, get *in* the Word, and get the Word *in* you. Then, much to God's delight, you will find yourself enjoying all the promises of God in your life, including prosperity and success in all that you do.

Moses told the children of Israel to remember throughout all their generations: "And you shall remember the LORD your God, for it is He who gives you power to get wealth, that He may establish His covenant which

He swore to your fathers, as it is this day" (Deuteronomy 8:18, NKJV). That's in the Bible in black and white. God, our father, is so wealthy, He paves the streets of heaven with gold. You may feel like all you can afford is asphalt, but in God's kingdom, the streets are pure gold.

King David wrote, "Let the LORD be magnified, who has pleasure in the prosperity of His servant" (Psalm 35:27, NKJV). He takes pleasure in your prosperity! David continues in Psalm 112, saying: "Blessed is the man who fears the LORD . . . his descendants will be mighty on earth; the generation of the upright will be blessed. Wealth and riches will be in his house . . ." (vv. 1–3, NKJV).

Wall Street cannot promise that! Politicians cannot promise that! Politicians have never given you anything that they didn't first take from someone else.

God Almighty has freely given to you ALL THINGS. St. Paul confirms this, saying, "Therefore let no one boast in men. For ALL THINGS ARE YOURS: whether Paul or Apollos or Cephas, or the world or life or death, or things present or things to come — ALL ARE YOURS" (1 Corinthians 3:21–22, NKJV, emphasis added).

PRINCIPLE TWO: GOD'S CHILDREN
HAVE HISTORICALLY BEEN PROSPEROUS

Remember the Golden Rule of Deuteronomy 8:18: it is the Lord — not Wall Street or your rich aunt — who gives you power to get wealth.

Genesis 13:2 records, "Abram was VERY RICH in cattle, in silver, and in gold" (KJV, emphasis added). I can assure you those three commodities are still the symbol of great wealth.

King David was rich and powerful, defeating Goliath, uniting Israel, conquering Jerusalem, gaining victory in every battle, and raising Solomon to be the wisest man who ever lived. He is the author of the blessing, "Peace be within thy walls, and prosperity within thy palaces" (Psalm 122:7, KJV). David was so wealthy he gave what in today's economy would amount to five million dollars in one offering. That's not bad for a fellow who started out with a slingshot and five rocks!

Don't believe that's in the Bible? Dust off your favorite translation and turn to 1 Chronicles 29. David has just told the people that his son, Solomon, has been chosen by God to be the next king and he will build the temple of the Lord. Solomon is still a child, however, so, like a proud father, David sets his son up for success by gathering all the materials that will be needed to build the temple. But he doesn't just stop there. David says,

"And now, because of my devotion to the Temple of my God, I am giving all of my own private treasures of gold and silver to help in the construction. This is in addition to the building materials I have already collected for his holy Temple. I am donating more than 112 tons of gold from Ophir and 262 tons of refined silver to be used for overlaying the walls of the buildings and for the other gold and silver work to be done by the craftsmen. Now then, who will follow my example and give offerings to the LORD today?" (1 Chronicles 29:3–5, NLT)

David had an abundance mindset. He gave $358,400,000 in gold alone to build the Temple. Valuing the price of gold at $2000 per ounce meant the value of 112 tons of gold equated to $358, 400, 000. Pricing silver at $126 per ounce meant David gave $217,984,000 to the Temple project in silver. The total gift: $517,384,000. Not bad for a shepherd.

This "man after God's own heart" was able to give all of his own private treasures, and to challenge others to be generous, because he knew from whence it came: "Everything we have has come from you, and we give you only what you first gave us!" (1 Chronicles 29:14, NLT). Everything comes from God. Everything you have God had first and He entrusted it to you. Even Job knew that God gives, and therefore God has the power to take away. So, everything you have to give is already God's. That is the only proper mindset to have when it comes to wealth.

Solomon's wealth was breathtaking. History records he was having gold and silver shipped into Israel from all over the known world. Archaeologists have discovered that the hinges on Solomon's horse stables were gold plated. With that kind of wealth, Solomon could have sent care packages to Bill Gates.

The Bible clearly states: "God is no respecter of persons" (Acts 10:34, KJV). If God allowed breathtaking wealth to be given to his children in the First Covenant . . . why not you?

PRINCIPLE THREE: GOD OWNS ALL THE WEALTH IN THE WORLD

The finest manual on the power to get wealth records these words: "For the kingdom of heaven is like a man traveling to a far country, who called his own servants and delivered **his goods** to them" (Matthew 25:14, NKJV, emphasis added).

There are two revolutionary concepts in this verse. First, the words "his goods" represent all the wealth of his kingdom, therefore he has the right to give whatever he desires to anyone at any time. There is a great deal of difference between rights and responsibilities. As the owner of all wealth, God has all the rights. You and I, as stewards of those goods, have responsibilities.

Secondly, since all the money is God's money, every spending decision is a spiritual decision. Your checkbook is a spiritual reflection of your love of God or your love for the things of this earth. Your checkbook is the mirror of your soul. An average family's checkbook looks like this: trip to Hawaii with the family, $20,000; tithes and offerings to the church, $15; special dog shampoo for your Goldendoodle, $75; donation to feed the poor, $20.

Remember that you are a steward and God is the owner. What does your checkbook say about you? Have you mismanaged God's money? What will you say to God on Judgment Day when you have invested more in your Goldendoodle than you have the Prince of Peace?

John Calvin said, "Where riches hold the dominion of the heart, God has lost His authority."[40]

PRINCIPLE FOUR: ALL GOD'S WEALTH BELONGS TO HIS CHILDREN

I once again point your attention to the greatest manual ever printed on the power to get wealth: "Therefore let no one boast in men. For all things are yours . . . And you are Christ's, and Christ is God's" (1 Corinthians 3:21–23, NKJV).

The greatest question you will ever answer is this: *Do you belong to Christ?* In other words, do you qualify to receive His wealth?

Romans 8:17 says, "and if children, then heirs — heirs of God and joint heirs with Christ" (NKJV). Think about it! Not equal heirs, meaning fifty-fifty, but joint heirs. "Joint heirs" means that all God has is mine and all I have is His. What a marvelous deal!

Consider the great exchange at the cross. I came to the cross saturated with poverty from the fall of man in Genesis; He gave me the riches of heaven and the blessings of Abraham. I gave Him my sins and He gave me wealth unlimited. I brought death through the curse of the Garden of Eden and He brought everlasting life. I brought sickness and disease; He brought divine health and healing, for He was and remains the Great Physician. I brought a life stained crimson red by sin; He washed me whiter than snow and forgave me of all my past forever. My past and yours were buried in the deepest sea never to be remembered anymore.

My friend, we got the best of that trade! Wealth is more than money; it is a relationship with God that maketh rich and addeth no sorrow. It's the peace of God that surpasses all understanding; it's joy unspeakable; it's hope for tomorrow the world didn't give it and the world can't take it away.

PRINCIPLE FIVE: JESUS PROFESSES HIS PERSONAL WEALTH

There are those who present Jesus Christ as poor and living hand-to-mouth when He was on this earth. That is absolute nonsense.

When Jesus was born, kings from the east brought trunks of gold to His birthplace. When a king brings you a chest full of gold you are not poor! Some kids are born with a silver spoon; Jesus was born with treasure chests of gold. Those kings came from five-hundred miles away. The Bible never says there were three of them. In fact, there was probably a whole band of them, blessing Jesus with enough to financially sponsor His ministry for the rest of his life.

Jesus had a home large enough for His friends to spend the night. This story is recorded in St. John 1:35–39. Jesus had finished teaching and his disciples followed him saying, "Rabbi, where are You staying? And He said to them, 'Come and see.' They came and saw where He was staying and remained with Him that day . . ." (vv. 37–39, NKJV). His house was big enough to accommodate those who were following Him.

After His ministry began, Jesus put Judas in charge of the money bag. You have to be doing alright to have enough money for your evangelistic team of twelve and still need a treasurer!

While He was nailed to the cross, Roman soldiers gambled for the seamless robe Jesus wore. They weren't being sentimental. They didn't love Jesus. They were doing their job as executioners and they saw how they could especially benefit from this one. That seamless robe had value, and they all wanted it.

The last picture we have of Jesus is not some shabby, trembly lip Holy Man in rags pushing all of His pathetic possessions in a shopping cart down the sidewalks of Jerusalem followed by His twelve ragged disciples singing, "Jesus, paid it all." The last picture we have of Jesus is by John the Revelator, saying: "Worthy is the Lamb, who was slain, to receive power *and wealth* and wisdom and strength and honor and glory and praise!" (Revelation 5:12, NIV, emphasis added).

When Jesus returns to earth to establish His final kingdom in Jerusalem, He's not going to be wrapped in swaddling clothes and laying in a cattle trough. He's going to come with enough diamonds to fence the entire city. His followers will not be taking the vow of poverty but will be wearing crowns of gold with dazzling white robes and living in mansions designed by the Architect of the Ages. Get that picture in your mind. If that's poverty, bring it on!

Those who advance the "poverty gospel" love to quote this verse: "Foxes have holes and birds of the air have nests, but the Son of Man has nowhere to lay His head" (Matthew 8:20, NKJV).

When interpreting Scripture, it is imperative to understand what the words of the text meant to the generation writing and first reading the text. The word Jesus used for "foxes" was referring to a people group known as the Idumaean Jews who were not one-hundred percent Jewish.

Jesus called Herod a fox when he said, "Go, tell that fox, 'Behold, I cast out demons and perform cures today and tomorrow, and the third day I shall be perfected'" (Luke 13:32, NKJV). In this verse, Jesus ridicules Herod and gives a powerful prophetic presentation of the future. The Bible says, "with the Lord one day is as a thousand years, and a thousand years as one day" (2 Peter 3:8, NKJV).

Jesus was saying that for two-thousand years His glorious Gospel would be preached, and demons would be cast out, and the sick would be healed; and on the third day (the beginning of the third thousand years), He would return to earth as King of Kings to rule the world in the Final Empire that would never end, from the city of Jerusalem, from a city whose beauty and wealth the mind of mortal flesh cannot comprehend.

To continue with the verse Jesus spoke, "Foxes have holes and birds of the air have nests, but the Son of Man has nowhere to lay His head", let's look at the word "birds." On the end of every Roman soldier's lance and shield was an eagle. Every building controlled by Rome had an eagle on it. The symbol of the eagle was everywhere.

Jesus was essentially saying, "The Roman invaders of the Holy Land have a place here, but the Creator of heaven and earth has no place on earth, because My kingdom is not of this world . . . My place is in the hearts of My people."

Christ rules the world through the hearts of those who follow Him. When He returns to Jerusalem, He will rule the world with a rod of iron and usher in the Golden Age of Perfect Peace.

PRINCIPLE SIX: INVEST IN YOURSELF

There are two words people routinely confuse: self-interest and selfishness. Self-interest is good; selfishness is a spiritual cancer.

It is in my self-interest to know the Lord. There are two choices for eternity: heaven and hell. You don't have to be a rocket scientist to know it's in your self-interest to go to heaven. And God earnestly wants you to choose accordingly.

It is in my self-interest to be happy. The Holy Scripture with its infinite wisdom has given us a signal for a long and productive life. The golden key that unlocks the door for a beautiful life reads: "A merry heart doeth good like a medicine" (Proverbs 17:22, KJV).

The Good Book continues with "the joy of the LORD is your strength" (Nehemiah 8:10, NKJV). It is in your self-interest to be joyful. Look for something to be happy about. Solomon, the wisest man on earth, said, "as he thinks in his heart, so is he" (Proverbs 23:7, NKJV). If all you allow your mind to think about are the bitter and hurtful experiences of your life, you will live miserable.

You can live in a gold-plated palace and be tormented by what you allow yourself to think about. If you are prone to focus on the bitterness of the past, you are allowing the past to control your future. Stop it!

Did you know that Jesus was a cheerleader? He said to those who followed Him, "Be of good cheer, I have overcome the world" (John 16:33, NKJV); "Be of good cheer; thy sins be forgiven thee" (Matthew 9:2, KJV); "Be of good cheer: it is I; be not afraid" (Mark 6:50, KJV).

You are responsible for what you allow yourself to think about. It is in your moments of decision that your destiny is determined. If you don't like something, change it. If you can't change it, change your attitude about it.

In His investment seminar, Jesus told His audience, "lay up for yourselves treasures in heaven, where neither moth nor rust destroys and where thieves do not break in and steal" (Matthew 6:20, ESV). I like to add: *and where the IRS cannot carry it off* (John Hagee Amplified Version)!

When Jesus was giving counsel to the rich young ruler in the Book of Matthew, He said, "And everyone who has left houses or brothers or sisters or father or mother or wife or children or lands, for My name's sake, shall receive a hundredfold, and inherit eternal life" (19:29, NKJV). That comma after hundredfold means that those blessings will take place in the here and now, IN THIS LIFE, *and* eternal life in the world to come.

Jesus said, "Give, and it shall be given unto you" (Luke 6:38, KJV). When you give, who gets the return? YOU! Let that sink in for a minute.

Chisel this concept into your brain: the day is coming when all you will have is what you have given to God. If all you had today was what you'd given God, what would you have? What would your bank account look like? What would your family look like?

If God wills it and you don't have it, that's not God's problem. God wants you to adjust your thinking to the fact that the promises of prosperity in the Bible apply to you.

PRINCIPLE SEVEN: GO TO WORK

God Almighty established the work principle. In the first chapter of the Book of Genesis, God worked six days creating the heavens and the earth.

When God gave the Ten Commandments in Exodus, they were not ten recommendations. One of those commandments reads: "Six days you shall WORK!"

St. Paul wrote to the New Testament Church: "If anyone will not work, neither shall he eat" (2 Thessalonians 3:10, NKJV). If America practiced this principle and withdrew all welfare cards from those who are healthy and refuse to work, we could balance the budget of this bankrupt country in short order.

My mother, a seminary graduate, had a work ethic that was off the charts. When I was eight years old, she took me to pick cotton in a southeast Texas cotton field owned by one of our church members. When I got out of the car, she gave me her Great Commission: "No son of mine is every going to be lazy . . . go to work!"

That cotton was as high as my head. It was hot, muggy, and I was dragging a twelve-foot sack. Picking cotton made every fingertips bleed in short order. We were paid one dollar for every hundred pounds that we picked. It took me two days to pick a dollar's worth.

When we moved from the country to Houston, Texas, she marched down to Weingarten's Supermarket located at the corner of Washington Avenue and Shephard Drive. There she tormented the manager until he gave me a job at the age of fourteen. I kept that job for years before going to the waterfront and working as a longshoreman in Houston, Texas.

I've had a full-time job since I was eight and therefore struggle to feel compassion for deadbeats who simply will not work.

Jesus clearly endorsed the work ethic in the teaching to his disciples of the three servants who were called in by their master (see Matthew 25). One was given five talents, a second was given two talents, and the third was given one talent. The servant who got five talents invested it and made five talents more. He now has ten talents. Jesus didn't reprimand him, saying, "You greedy capitalist, don't you feel compassion for those who won't work?" He did say, "Well done, thou good and faithful servant" (v. 21, NKJV).

The story gets better! The second servant invested two talents and made two talents more. Now he had four and Jesus congratulated him for his efforts.

The third servant, Howard the Coward, who got one talent, dug a hole and hid it. Jesus's response was, "You wicked and lazy servant" (v. 26, NKJV). Jesus immediately took the one talent away from the servant who buried his talent and gave it to the investor who doubled his talents from five to ten.

Had Jesus been a liberal politician running for office in America, He would have said, "You poor millennialist baby, you've been disadvantaged. You've graduated from Harvard, and at thirty-five you're still living in your mother's basement. Not to worry, we'll tax the rich guy who worked his brains out and made ten talents and redistribute the wealth and punish those who succeed. Because you are entitled to more."

Jesus was no socialist. He would not stand for an "entitlement" approach to life that refuses to work, nor for celebrity parents who pay bribes to get their children into the best schools, nor people gaming the unemployment system simply because they can make more that way than they can getting a job. You deserve nothing until you work for it!

My friend, you may "receive" unemployment, but you "earn" a paycheck. You aren't entitled to it. It's not a gift. It's an exchange of value. Sweat for money. You work hard and you *earn* it. By Jesus's own efforts, He worked as a carpenter's son and commended all He met who took their God-given talents and produced a rich return.

PRINCIPLE EIGHT: GIVER'S GAIN

It is an indisputable fact in American history that many of those who were truly rich gave abundantly to the less fortunate, and in doing so, made their lives a more joyful journey.

In his lifetime, John D. Rockefeller donated over five-hundred million dollars to charity.

J.C. Penney, whose first store was called "The Golden Rule," also donated millions in his later years.[41]

When William Colgate moved to New York at the age of sixteen, he told the captain of the boat he was on that he was going to make soap. The captain told him if he wanted to be the biggest and the best soap manufacturer then he had to follow this advice: "Begin by tithing all you receive." William Colgate founded the Colgate-Palmolive Company and always tithed more than ten percent of his earnings. William Colgate died in 1857 but his company and his legacy are a success to this day.[42] At the age of 80, I still brush my teeth every morning with Colgate toothpaste.

Chuck Feeney, who made his fortune establishing a line of duty-free airport shops in 1960, finally met his financial goal in December 2016: to give away his fortune while he was still alive. He said, "I had one idea that never changed in my mind — that you should use your wealth to help people."[43]

The two most generous philanthropists in the United States today, Warren Buffett and Bill Gates, formed "The Giving Pledge," encouraging the "haves" to donate the bulk of their wealth to worthy causes. Buffett says, "If you're in the luckiest one-percent of humanity, you owe it to the rest of humanity to think about the other ninety-nine percent."[44]

These men may not be followers of Christ, but they give and give and give, and have a great time doing it!

Everything that God ordains, gives. The sun that God created on the Genesis morning gives light to the world, without which life would not be possible. The stars give guidance. The soil produces plants to give us food. The clouds give rain and the rainbow gives hope.

God gave His only begotten Son to redeem us and give us hope for the future. Jesus gave His life.

The twelve disciples gave their lives to fulfill the Great Commission. St. Paul gave his life to bring the Good News to the Gentiles and the New Testament believers.

If something within you resents giving, that something is not from God.

God has created a world where it is not possible to receive something without giving something. Giving is the only proof you have that greed has not become a cancer on your soul.

Think about it. When you go to your favorite department store and find a shirt you like, what do you do? You carry the shirt to the register and hand the salesperson some money. He or she keeps the money and gives you a plastic bag with your new shirt inside. Next thing you know you are out the door without setting off any alarm bells.

Those alarm bells are the key, because if you receive without giving, it's called shoplifting.

Many Christians are shoplifting their way through church. They come to church on Sunday morning to receive without giving anything in return. They come to get healed, to have their marriages saved, their children straightened out, and their businesses put back on course. Yet when that offering plate passes, they avoid eye contact. They mutter something about giving online. They put in a widow's mite even though they've just received their year-end bonus.

Have you heard of the Pareto principle? This is the 80/20 rule, and unfortunately it applies to churches, not just economies. This principle says that eighty percent of the output comes from twenty percent of the input. In other words, eighty percent of the load is carried by twenty percent of the people.

Studies show that this applies to giving as well: less than twenty-five percent of church goers tithe ten percent of their income. The majority of Christians only give 2.5 percent of their income as a tithe — down from 3.3 percent during the Great Depression![45] Those studies weren't done while the nation was shut down in 2020 over the coronavirus pandemic. Those studies weren't done during the financial crisis of 2009. Those studies were done in an average year, revealing that Christians are doing a far-below average job of walking in the power of God to get wealth. Imagine what we could do if one hundred percent of us pitched in and did exactly what God has called us to do?

The Bible principle is very clear: "Give, and it shall be given unto you" (Luke 6:38, KJV). Until you give, you don't qualify to receive the power to get wealth.

Peter Marshall was the Chaplain of the United States Senate in the late 1940s. A man came to him with a concern about the tithe. He told Dr. Marshall, "I have a problem. I've been tithing for some time. It wasn't too bad when I started out working. I was making twenty-thousand dollars a year and I could afford to give two thousand. But, you see, I'm now making five-hundred thousand a year, and there's just no way that I can afford a tithe of fifty-thousand dollars."

Dr. Marshall reflected on the man's dilemma and said, "Yes, sir, I think you do have a problem. I think what we ought to do is pray right now. Would that be okay?" The man agreed. So, Dr. Marshall bowed his head, put his hand on the man's shoulder and prayed with boldness and authority: "Dear Lord, this man has a problem. I pray that you help him, Lord. I pray that you reduce his salary back to the place where he can afford to tithe."[46]

The next time the offering plate comes around, see it as your opportunity to prosper. Recognize that the decision you are about to make will determine your financial future.

The second part of Luke 6:38 says, "For with the measure you use it will be measured back to you" (ESV). The New Living Translation says it this way, "The amount you give will determine the amount you get back." If you give liberally, God will open the windows of heaven and bless you with blessings that cannot be contained. That's a fact.

God longs to bless you with a tidal wave of blessings, but He cannot bless what hasn't been given. Deuteronomy 28:2 says, "And all these blessings shall come upon you and overtake you, if you obey the voice of the LORD your God" (ESV). You don't get the "then" without the "if." But "if" you've got the "if" — "if" you obey God, "then" hold on because God is about to blow open the storehouses!

You'll be blessed in the city and blessed in the country, blessed at work and blessed at home, blessed in your finances and blessed in your refrigerators, blessed amongst friends and blessed amongst your enemies. I like the way Eugene Peterson puts it: ". . . you'll always be the top dog, never the bottom dog, as you obediently listen to and diligently keep the commands of God, your God" (Deuteronomy 28:13, MSG). Hot dog!

PRINCIPLE NINE:
GO "THERE," TO THE PLACE OF PROVISION

First Kings 17 tells the story of Elijah and the widow of Zarephath. There was a famine in the land, and a time of drought. There was so little water that even the brooks had dried up. God told Elijah to go to Zarephath where a widow would take care of him. People were starving. They were dying of dehydration.

But God was clear: Go "there," and I will meet your needs (see 1 Kings 17:7–16). If Elijah expected to find a wealthy widow with a doomsdayer's bunker full of food, he was sorely mistaken. God didn't send Elijah to the widow because of what she had, but because of what God wanted to do.

Elijah went "there" — to the exact place that God told him to go — and he was fed. Had Elijah gone next door or to a different village or looked for someone better off than the widow of Zarephath, he would have starved to death. But he went "there" — to the exact place God specified for him to go.

San Antonio, Texas, is my "there." Over fifty-five years ago, God called me to plant a church in San Antonio. It was not my idea. I might have picked Dallas, or at least Houston, but not San Antonio. But I went "there," and God has grown this ministry through His power and blessing.

God has an exact place for you, and when you get "there," miracles are going to happen. Every dimension of your life will increase. Sickness and disease will be defeated. Financial breakthrough will come suddenly — maybe not immediately, but most definitely suddenly. Family relationships will come under divine harmony.

Mountains of impossibility will be cast into the sea. Fear will surrender to faith. You will feel like you are in the fiery furnace when suddenly the fourth man appears, and you walk out of it without even the smell of smoke upon you. When you walk in obedience to God into the place of His purpose, He will meet all your needs with power.

The widow knew that making bread for Elijah would mean no last supper for her son, yet she obeyed. She made bread for Elijah, and he ate it. Right in front of those starving people, he ate every last bite. Imagine the headlines: "Widow and Son Starve to Death when Preacher Eats their Last Taco."

But then the miraculous happened. The widow got up and made some bread for herself and her son. Every day she made bread, because her flour miraculously did not run out, and her jug of olive oil did not run dry. Because Elijah went "there," and the widow went "there," they had abundance in a time of poverty. The power to get wealth.

This incredible story isn't over. Three years later, the story resumes. Elijah, the widow, and her son have been well-nourished this whole time because of that single seed of obedience that was planted.

After three years without rain in Israel, God promised Elijah that rain was coming. Israel was a nation of farmers. When you're a farmer and there is no rain, there are no crops. If there are no crops, there is no food, no money, and the people starve. This was a dire situation, a national crisis. God told Elijah that rain was coming, but first he had to go to Ahab, the king of Israel.

Ahab was married to a woman named Jezebel who was killing God's preachers for sport. They were hiding out in caves to keep away from her. She was making a bad situation worse. So Elijah went to Ahab and said, bring your prophets — the 450 prophets of Baal and the 400 prophets of Asherah — and we'll have a theological shoot-out. Your prophets will sacrifice a bull and call on your god. I'll sacrifice a bull and call on my God. And whichever god answers by fire is the real God. May the best god win! (See 1 Kings 18.)

Let me say this candidly: Christianity in America must learn to confront evil. We have become entirely too soft. When we see evil, we should call it what it is and not blink. There is only one God, and there is only one way to Him; and if we see anything even slightly off course, we must shout it down! If the devil wants a fight, give him one because our God wins every time.

I just gave away the ending, but I'm still going to tell you the rest of the story because it's a good one. Elijah tells the prophets of Baal to sacrifice a bull and to call on Baal to light a fire under it. Those prophets called and called. All day they called and called. Elijah taunted them, telling them they weren't shouting loud enough. When he wasn't looking, they probably poured lighter fluid on that bull but still there was no fire.

Now it was Elijah's turn. He prepared the bull and put it on the altar. But instead of praying, he asked the people who had gathered around to pour water all over the offering. Now remember, this is a time of famine, a time of drought. So, Elijah told them to use up the one thing they lacked.

He told them to pour four jars of water on the offering and on the wood. Then he told them to pour four more, and four more. They poured enough water to fill a trench around the altar. All those thirsty people dumping water in the dirt. Why? Because Elijah was sowing what God had promised. God promised rain, so Elijah sowed the last bit of water they had: twelve barrels, one barrel for each of the twelve tribes of Israel.

Giving is sewing what you have been given to create what you have been promised.

After twelve jars of water had been poured out on the altar, Elijah prayed to God to bring fire to the water-soaked wood. Boom! A roaring fire came down and swallowed up the bull, the wood, and the water. Gone! All the people watching fell on their faces and praised God, the one true God, the Name above all names, the Almighty Savior. Yes and amen!

When you ask God for something, think big. Elijah didn't just want enough water to fill a thermos, he was asking for a blessing upon the entire nation of Israel. When you ask God for something, pour out the thing you are asking for. Give what you need. Elijah needed water, so he poured out water. If you need love from your spouse, pour out love on your spouse. If you need friendship, be a friend. If you need finances, give of your finances.

This is not at all how we think, but this is how God works. We think, *I need money, so I shouldn't tithe this month.* We think, *I need love, so I'm going to be a grouch until I get it.* We think, *I need more, so I'm going to hoard what I've got.* But in God's economy, if you want it, you've got to sow it. Give what you've got, and then you'll get what you want.

After Elijah poured out the twelve precious barrels of water, he told Ahab to go and feast because a heavy downpour was coming. And that's exactly what happened. The skies turned black. The winds picked up. And the rains came down and soaked the nation of Israel, reviving the national economy instantly.

PRINCIPLE TEN: GIVING CREATES A MEMORIAL

The final principle of the power to get wealth is that acts of generosity create *memorials.* Just before the crucifixion, Mary broke an alabaster box of expensive perfume over the head of Jesus, anointing Him for burial. The precious spikenard would have cost her a year's wages. This act of giving was her love poured out for Him.

It was a sacrifice that took mere seconds, but has been remembered for centuries: "Assuredly, I say to you, wherever this gospel is preached in the whole world, what this woman has done will also be told as a memorial to her" (Matthew 26:13, NKJV). Giving creates a memorial before God that He never forgets.

I'm bringing Mary to your remembrance today in fulfillment of what Jesus said prophetically two thousand years ago. Her gift created, in the kingdom of God, an eternal memorial. The rich aroma of that twelve ounces of spikenard soaked into the beard and the body and the seamless robe of the Son of God. It filled the room. Jesus was not alone in the last forty-eight hours of His life. His robe was soaked with the aroma of Mary's sacrificial, memorial gift.

When Jesus prayed in the Garden of Gethsemane and His disciples went to sleep, the aroma was there. When Jesus stood before Pilate and the people cried out, "We have no king but Caesar," that powerful aroma was there.

When He was whipped by the Roman cat of nine tails and His blood ran into the streets, that rich aroma was there to remind Him that someone loved Him enough to give their very best for Him. When His hands and feet were nailed to the cross, when He felt forsaken by even His own Father, the aroma was there.

When you give, you too are creating a memorial that says to God — the One who gave His very best for you — that you are willing to do your very, very best for Him. Are you giving God your best?

– FIVE –

THE POWER OF COMMUNICATION

"Not only do men and women communicate differently but they think, feel, perceive, react, respond, love, need, and appreciate differently. They almost seem to be from different planets, speaking different languages and needing different nourishment." -JOHN GRAY[47]

"The single biggest problem in communication is the illusion that it has taken place." -GEORGE BERNARD SHAW[48]

"What we have here is a failure to communicate." That's the famous line uttered by the prison warden in the iconic Paul Newman movie, *Cool Hand Luke*.

Communication is defined as "the imparting or exchanging of information."[49] That sounds simple enough, but how many of you have ever been misunderstood? Men, how many of you have ever told your wife something as clearly as you can speak, and she got it all wrong?

Ladies, how many of you have told your husband something as clearly as you can explain, and he got it wrong, wrong, wrong? We have developed communication systems that permit people on the earth to talk to people walking on the moon, yet we have husbands who can't talk to their wives, mothers who can't talk to their daughters, fathers who can't talk to their sons across the kitchen table.

Problems and differences in marriage, family, business, friendships, and other relationships are not dangerous. But not being able to openly communicate about those problems is very dangerous.

Communication is when a husband and wife can honestly tell each other who they are, what they want, how they feel, what they love, what they honor, what they esteem, what they hate, what they fear, what they desire, what they hope for, what they believe in, and what they are committed to. Then, and only then, does true communication take place.

Too many couples have called it quits, claiming they grew apart when really, they simply stopped communicating. They may have continued talking, yelling, slamming doors, and the like, but they stopped communicating clearly, effectively, and from the heart.

In this chapter we will explore clear communication, communication killers, steps to effective communication, and two powerful expressions that you cannot live without.

LET'S BE CLEAR

The story goes that a man called his neighbor to help him move a couch that had become stuck in his doorway. The men pushed and pulled until they were exhausted, but the couch wouldn't budge. Exasperated, the couch's owner finally said, "Forget it. We'll never get this thing in the house." The neighbor looked at him and said, "In?"[50]

Communication, whether it's in marriage, business, the church, or personal relationships, must be absolutely clear to be effective.

Have you ever played the game Telephone, where one person relays information to the next person who relays to the next person and so forth until you get to the last person who has to share what they've heard? Let me give you an illustration.

A school superintendent told his assistant superintendent the following: "Next Thursday morning at 10:30, Haley's Comet will appear over this area. It's an event that happens every seventy-five years. Call the school principals and have them assemble the teachers and the classes on the athletic field to explain this phenomenal event. If it rains, cancel the day's observation and have the classes meet in the auditorium to see a film on the comet."

The assistant superintendent sent this communication to the school principals: "By order of the superintendent, next Thursday at 10:30, Haley's Comet will appear over your athletic field. If it rains, cancel the day's classes and report to the auditorium where you'll be shown a film of a phenomenal event that happens every seventy-five years at our school."

The principals then relayed this information to the teachers: "By order of the phenomenal superintendent, at 10:30 next Thursday, Haley's Comet will be appearing in our auditorium. In case of rain over the athletic field, the superintendent will give another order, something that only happens every seventy-five years."

The teachers sent this communication to the students: "Next Thursday at 10:30, the superintendent of the schools will appear in the school auditorium with Haley's Comet, something that occurs here only every seventy-five years. If it rains, the superintendent will cancel the comet and order us out to our phenomenal athletic field."

The students went home and shared with their parents: "When it rains next Thursday at 10:30 over the school athletic field, our seventy-five-year-old superintendent will cancel all the classes, and he's going to appear in the auditorium with Bill Haley and the Comets."

The joke is funny, but sadly it illustrates a truth that is all too real in many relationships: we don't know how to communicate.

The Bible is a remarkable book in many respects, but one of these is how clearly it communicates truth and wisdom. Thou shalt not lie. Thou shalt not commit adultery. Thou shalt not steal. Thou shalt not use the name of the Lord thy God in vain. Thou shalt not have any other gods before me. Thou shalt do no murder. Thou shalt not bear false witness. What clarity and simplicity! What part of "thou shalt not" is unclear?

It is impossible to be confused by this! This is not "clear as mud" like my mother used to say. This is clear and very clear. The Bible says the way is so simple that even a fool "shall not err therein" (Isaiah 35:8, KJV). The only way you can misunderstand that book is by not reading it.

Saint Paul wrote to the New Testament Church, "Now I would not have you ignorant, brethren . . ." (Romans 1:13, KJV). Of course, a misplaced comma could turn that into: "I would not have you, ignorant brethren." Commas are important in communication, too!

A WORD FITLY SPOKEN

We find a compelling illustration of the power of communication — both good and bad — in the story of Nabal and Abigail in 1 Samuel 25. There we discover that Abigail knew the power of "a word fitly spoken" (see Proverbs 25:11–12, NKJV), but her husband Nabal was a rotten, worm-infested apple. In fact, his name means "fool." I don't know who his parents were, but they did not set him up for success with a name like that.

Now, by the world's standards, Nabal was successful. He had three thousand sheep and a thousand goats. Yet here we have a stark reminder that possessing all the money in the world won't compensate for possessing a fool's heart!

This incident transpired during the season young David was on the run from Saul — a jealous king with murder on his mind. But David wasn't alone. He had a loyal private army with him, and they were stronger than any nation. So, David sent some of his men to Nabal to ask him properly and politely to show David and his men hospitality. But Nabal responded like the brute he was and said, "not happening vagabonds." David immediately strapped on his sword and made plans to wipe out every one of Nabal's men.

Enter Abigail. She gets wind of what her knot head of a husband has done, and immediately springs into action.

I imagine this was not the first time she had been forced to come to his rescue. She saddles up a donkey and heads straight for David and his men. As soon as she finds them, she falls prostrate on the ground before David and begins to skillfully use words to douse the fire her husband's foolish words had ignited: "Master," "Lord," "blessed of God . . ." These simple words communicate clearly to David the respect and conciliatory posture needed to calm the gathering storm.

Abigail continues: ". . . please let your maidservant speak in your ears, and hear the words of your maid-servant" (v. 24, NKJV). She is clever. She knows how to get his attention: "Don't dwell on what that brute Nabal did. He acts out the meaning of his name: Nabal, Fool. Foolishness oozes from him" (v. 25, MSG). Foolishness was such a part of Nabal that it seeped out of his pores and into every word that he spoke.

Abigail goes on to tell David that she knows how powerful and successful he is, and how he does battle on behalf of the Lord. The linchpin in the whole encounter is her insightful observation, "the Lord has held you back from coming to bloodshed and from avenging yourself with your own hand" (v. 26, NKJV). Once again, Abigail is clear: *God sent me to protect you from acting foolish like my husband. God is on your side. You aren't killing anyone today, future king!*

Nabal dies a fool, and Abigail becomes David's new first lady. The power of communication!

COMMUNICATION KILLERS

A man said to his friend, "My wife and I had words last night. I just didn't get a chance to use mine."

I believe there are "communication killers" that prevent the clear, effective communication that is necessary for us to have successful relationships. Let's take a look at the top five.

The first communication killer is *fear.* Communication blooms in the soil of trust. When one spouse tries to force their point of view on the other, you have an emotional dictatorship. Interestingly, it is often not the strongest person in the relationship who pushes their point of view on the other, but rather the most insecure party. Insecure people are dogmatic; they can't be wrong. They are too emotionally weak to allow anyone to disagree with them.

Manipulation, domination, and intimidation are, in reality, forms of witchcraft. Did you know that it's possible to sing "Amazing Grace" in church on Sunday and practice witchcraft in your marriage the other six days each week? If you demand that your spouse agree with you in everything, you are denying them an emotional and intellectual life of their own.

Healthy, effective communication requires emotional nakedness; but that's impossible where dominance and insecurity are present. In order to expose yourself to another person, you need to first know that you will be heard, respected, and not made to feel ashamed or foolish.

Do you ridicule your spouse? Do you speak sarcastically to the love of your life, or *about* them to others in their presence? Are you full of perpetual rage? Do you say things like, "You don't look as good as you used to"? Let me ask you, "Who does?"

Don't be average. The average man is around forty years of age, forty-eight around the waist, 120 around the golf course, and a nuisance around the house. Between Mary Kay and Victoria's Secret, the average woman is buried alive under false eyelashes and wonder bras. Before I get myself into even deeper trouble, let's move on to the second communication killer.

I'm talking about a *lack of honesty*. Have you ever twisted the facts so that they were compatible with your point of view? How does that work in real life?

Two boys were playing football in a park in a small Texas town when one of the boys was suddenly attacked by a crazed pit bull. Thinking quickly, the other boy took a stick and shoved it in the dog's collar. He twisted the stick and broke the dog's neck, saving his friend's life.

A sportswriter who was walking by witnessed the incident. He came over to interview the boy. Flipping open his reporter's notepad, he told the boy he was going to write a story for the newspaper.

He said he was going to title the article, "Young Texas Longhorn Fan Saves Friend from Vicious Animal." The little boy protested, "But I'm not a Longhorn fan." The sportswriter said, "Well, everybody in Texas is either a Longhorn fan or a Texas Aggie. So I'll headline the article, 'Fighting Texas Aggie Rescues Friend from Horrific Attack.' How does that sound?" The boy said, "I don't like that either." The sportswriter said, "Well, why not?" The boy said, "Because I'm from Oklahoma and I think the Oklahoma Sooners are the greatest football team in America." The sportswriter frowned, tore off a sheet on his notepad, and started writing a new title: "Little Redneck Savage from Oklahoma Kills Beloved Family Pet."

That's what you call twisting the facts to support your preferred narrative. Be honest.

A third communication killer is the *angry explosion*. When I think about that principle, I'm reminded of a married couple who were celebrating their fiftieth wedding anniversary with friends and family. Someone asked them the secret of their success, and the husband replied, "We agreed when we got married that, when I got mad, I would go outside. We also agreed that when she got mad,

I would also go outside. So, the secret of our marriage is, for the past fifty years I've been outside!"

It's a proven fact that deep feelings must be expressed, one way or another. Think of it like trying to hold a beach ball under the water. You can wrestle with it, move side to side with it, even try to sit on it, but eventually it will explode to the surface like Mount Vesuvius. Just like that beach ball, all of your deeply felt emotions that are not expressed in a healthy way will sooner or later erupt. And trust me, it won't be pretty.

A fourth communication killer is *tears.* I know both men and women who have used this tactic effectively. If during the first spat a newlywed couple has the wife turns on the water works, she is teaching her husband that there is a line he cannot cross, or she'll cry. At that moment, communication stops, and control begins.

The fifth communication killer is *exaggeration.* You've heard the tragic story of the boy who cried wolf. Well, let me tell you the story of a boy who cried "lion." He was six years old when he ran into the house screaming, "Mother, there's a cat in the backyard that's as big as a lion!" The mother scolded the little boy and said, "If I've told you once, I've told you a hundred times; stop exaggerating!"

She sent him to his room and told him to ask the Lord to help him with his exaggeration problem. Ten minutes later, the boy came out of his room. His mother said, "Well?" The little boy said, "I talked to God about it. And He told me that the first time He saw that cat, He thought it was a lion, too!"

Fear, lack of honesty, angry explosion, tears, and exaggeration. These are communication killers. But I've also come across some "power tools" for effective communication that will help improve every relationship in your life.

EFFECTIVE COMMUNICATION

Strangling good communication is the easy part. Anyone can do that. The hard job is learning to communicate effectively. And as with every job, having the right plan or blueprint is vital. I've discovered that healthy, effective communication can be achieved in seven steps.

Step One: *Employ empathy*, or what I like to call "The Ezekiel Method."

Empathy is the capacity to feel what another person is feeling. This is most common when you have experienced exactly what they are experiencing. By the way, never say to someone, "I know what you're going through," unless you have actually gone through what they are going through and have experienced the loss they are experiencing.

Husband, don't tell your wife you understand her. You don't. You're just trying to get out of the room! Don't tell someone who has lost a child that you get it because your beloved family dog died last year. You don't get anything. Don't tell someone whose parent is suffering from dementia that you wish your own mother would forget who you were sometimes. That's not lovingkindness.

The best thing you can do for someone whose circumstances you haven't experienced is to wrap your arms around them, hold them, and say, "I love you and I'm here for you. I may not know how your feeling, but I'll walk through this with you." Why do I call this The Ezekiel Method?

In the third chapter of Ezekiel, the prophet said, "I sat where they sat" (Ezekiel 3:15, NKJV). There was a concentration camp of Israelites being held in Babylon as slaves. They'd lost their homes. They'd lost their freedom. They'd lost their destiny. They'd lost all hope. David reflected, "Beside the rivers of Babylon, we sat and wept as we thought of Jerusalem" (Psalm 137:1, NLT).

Ezekiel wanted to communicate with the Israelites. He had a word from the Lord for them. So, for seven days, he simply sat where they sat.

No one wants optimism from an armchair quarterback. No one wants glib words of wisdom from a long-haired prophet who has no scars on his back. Ezekiel knew that, so instead of going into their camp with guns blazing and spewing forth prophecies and platitudes, he shut up and took a seat. He became one of them. He lived with the Israelites in captivity. He experienced firsthand the humiliation they were experiencing. He walked in their shoes, looked at the world through their eyes, and felt what they were feeling.

The Ezekiel Method is simply seeing from another's point of view. Husbands and wives can do this. Bosses and employees can do this. Wise counselors recommend it.

One of the shortest counseling sessions I ever had involved The Ezekiel Method. A husband came in who obviously had little appreciation for his wife, who was taking care of three small children without any help in a crowded house. So I said to him, "Take a day and sit where she sits. Stay home all day with your three small children. And while you are there, clean the house, wash the dishes, cook the meals, mop the floors, wash and iron the clothes, change the diapers, potty train the littlest one, answer the phone, get the groceries, and have a wonderful supper on the table when your wife gets home. Oh, and make sure you look as fresh as a daisy, happy, and well-rested with a passion in your eyes for your wife." John Wayne didn't give me a second look. He went and found another counselor.

All kidding aside, you can't truly understand a person or their situation until you see it from their perspective.

I think doctors are wonderful people. I've seen more of them than I want to in the past few years of my life. Those experiences have left me thinking every doctor should be sick just once. They should be admitted to the hospital under the name "John Doe" where they work and see it from their patients' perspective. Every doctor should be awakened at midnight for a blood pressure check, and at 2:00 a.m. with a six-inch needle in the behind, and again at 4:00 a.m. just to see if they are resting well.

Police officers are also wonderful people, but every officer should be given a ticket by another officer who spends their day hiding behind a bush with a radar gun next to a sign that says: "Reduce speed ahead."

Have you ever watched people walk down the street and pass by a destitute beggar with a tin cup? I'm not talking about some young hustler who's looking for a shortcut to holding down a real job. I'm talking about somebody who desperately needs the help. The people who give are the ones who know what it feels like to need something and not be able to get it themselves.

Oh Lord, help me to never judge another person until I have walked in their shoes for two weeks!

Jesus Christ so loved the world that He came to earth to sit where you sit, to feel what you feel. Why do we pray to God the Father in Jesus's name? Because Jesus is the only person in heaven who knows how a human being feels. He came to earth and became one of us. He was a minority, hated as a Jewish person. He was rejected. He was criticized.

He was betrayed by His friends, Judas and Peter. He was falsely accused by the church and the state. The state said He was an insurrectionist, too dangerous to live. The church said He was a heretic and a demonized teacher. He was physically abused, beaten, and crucified. He was murdered, even though He was innocent. You can't ever say that no one understands what you are going through, because Jesus does. Jesus, the Son of God, understands, because He has sat where you sit. Talk to Him! He knows what you are going through.

The second step is to communicate with *a compassionate touch.*

True compassion is often transmitted through touch. As I write this book, the world is in a state of panic over the Coronavirus pandemic. We've been told by the directors of our state health departments not to come within six feet of one another. For many, it has been months since they have shaken hands, patted one another on the back, given hugs, or expressed any sort of compassion through physical touch. We can't even smile at one another because our faces are covered in masks. I can only imagine the psychological damage this is doing to us as a people.

On the other hand, it has forced families to spend more time together — time that truly could strengthen the nuclear family which has seen such a decline in recent decades. The pandemic is slowing down many parents who had fully abandoned themselves to the rat race of life. It's arresting and redirecting couples who had grown too busy to touch each other, to hug their children, to hold the people they love.

Studies in pre-pandemic times reported that American families spent a mere thirty-seven minutes of quality time together per day.[51] And that fathers spent less than twenty seconds a day talking to their teenage sons.[52] That is a crisis of biblical proportions that I just can't comprehend.

Every time I see my kids, I hug them. They are adults ranging from age thirty-nine to fifty, but still I hug them every time. On one occasion, when my kids were younger, my son John Christopher got out of the house before I had the chance to hug and kiss him and tell him to have a good day.

So I drove to the bus stop and got out of the car. John Christopher saw me coming and started running. He was screaming, "No! No!" He knew what was coming and he didn't want me to kiss him in front of all his friends. I was chasing him down the street while the neighbors threatened to call the cops. I could run back then so I caught up to John Christopher and hugged him and kissed him and told him to have a good day. Then I got back in my car and went to work.

Touch is so powerful. There are thirteen-hundred nerve endings per square inch in your hands.[53] Each nerve ending, when touched, sends a message to your brain. That's why one touch is worth a thousand words.

Touch is the magic wand of intimacy. Husbands, when you touch your wives, you are communicating a thousand words. You are telling her you understand, you love her, you appreciate her, you are listening to her. Wives, when you touch your husbands, you are communicating that you are proud of him, that you appreciate him, that you honor him, that you desire him. All that with a single touch!

Jesus showed compassion with the power of touch. One touch from Jesus could heal a person from death and disease and cleanse them from all sin and unrighteousness.

One of the most powerful stories of Jesus's healing is in the Book of Matthew:

> When He had come down from the mountain, great multitudes followed Him. And behold, a leper came and worshiped Him, saying, "Lord, if You are willing, you can make me clean." Then Jesus put out His hand and touched him, saying, "I am willing; be cleansed." Immediately his leprosy was cleansed. (Matthew 8:1–3, NKJV)

Though given but a few verses, this scene speaks volumes. The man, with great faith, asks Jesus to heal him from the skin condition that made him an outcast everywhere he went, even among his own family. He was an outcast not only because he was diseased, but because of the belief that his "uncleanness" was contagious. Whether or not a person could actually contract leprosy by being in contact with the man was perhaps less important than the belief that touching him would make one "unclean" — in other words, the sin that they believed had caused his leprosy would rub off on them.

The leper says to Jesus, "If You are willing, You can make me clean." He knew that Jesus was *able*, "You *can* make me clean." But was he *willing*?

Jesus was willing: "Then Jesus put out His hand and touched him, saying, 'I am willing; be cleansed'." More than His willingness to cleanse the man, Jesus communicated compassion by reaching out and touching the man who hadn't been touched, who hadn't been allowed within six feet of anyone, for God knows how long.

That touch, that one act of compassion, healed more than the man's skin condition. It healed his heart and spoke volumes to the crowd of people who were witnesses to it.

The third step to effective communication is to *communicate with love*. The Bible says in Ephesians 4:15, "speak the truth in love" (NLT), and by doing so you become more like Christ. The more truth you speak, the more love you should convey. Truth is like a two-edged sword; be careful how you wield it!

Nothing improves a wife's hearing like the sound of praise. Proverbs 31:28 says, "Her children rise up and call her blessed; her husband also, and he praises her" (NKJV). Husbands, do you praise your wife? Once, twenty years ago, doesn't count! Have you praised her TODAY?

Are you as courteous to your wife as you are the next-door neighbor? Or is it more natural for you to complain rather than to compliment? Let me tell you something about complaints and compliments. All compliments should be public. All complaints should be private — very, very private!

When Mark was in school, his math teacher gave the class an unusual assignment. She asked them to write down the names of each of their classmates, and then beside each name they were to write down the nicest thing they could think of about each one. She then compiled the compliments and gave each student his or her own list.

Years later, Mark was killed in Vietnam. Amongst those who attended his funeral was that math teacher. Mark's father approached the teacher after the service and, pulling a folded sheet of notebook paper out of his wallet, showed her the list of compliments Mark had been given in her classroom. He'd had it on him all those years later when he died.[54] You never know the lasting effect a compliment may have on a person's life.

David wrote in Psalm 19, "Let the words of my mouth, and the meditation of my heart, be acceptable in thy sight, O LORD, my strength, and my redeemer" (Psalm 19:14, KJV). A word spoken in love will always be acceptable to the Lord.

The fourth step to effective communication is to *allow for reaction time.* This is so important.

When you initiate a difficult conversation with someone, please remember that you had the advantage of thinking about what you were going to say in advance. You had time to prepare, to ponder. You may even have anticipated the other person's response: *If he says this, I'll say that; if she says that, I'll say this.* Point, counterpoint. You had time to mentally rehearse. But the person you approach may be taken completely off guard.

They may have an initial reaction, but you should also allow for a later I've-had-time-to-think-about-it response. Especially if you caught them at a vulnerable moment. None of us can be responsible for what we say when we are hungry or tired! When I'm tired, I'll say anything just so I can go to bed or get out of the conversation. But the next morning, that's when I want to hit the rewind button and say what I should have said.

The fifth step to effective communication is to *pray together and for each other.* The Bible says, "do not let the sun go down on your wrath" (Ephesians 4:26, NKJV). Do you know how hard it is to pray for your spouse when you are truly angry with them? Start praying and the anger will subside and lead you to reconciliation.

There is no distance in prayer. God can bring together that which has been injured or broken. The words that separated you can bring you back together again. If you can't pray together, pray for one another, and one day you'll be holding hands and saying the Lord's Prayer together with a peace in your heart that can only be explained by the power of God.

The sixth step to effective communication is to *share the details*. One day a husband was reading the morning paper when an article reported that a new study proved women use more words than men. The husband, who frequently accused his wife of talking too much, showed his wife the article, excited to prove his point.

The article stated, "Men use about 15,000 words per day, but women use 30,000." The wife glanced at the article then returned the paper to her husband, saying, "That's because we have to repeat everything we say." Caught off guard, the husband said, "What?"[55]

There is a saying: *Happy wife, happy life.* You might have heard it this way: "If momma ain't happy, ain't nobody happy!" Either way, this will make the ladies happy when I say this next part: when it comes to details, men need to learn from their wives.

Women are so much better at details than men. I hate details. I want to bypass everything and get straight to the point. My wife, on the other hand, has a PhD in details. When I get home, she asks, "How was your day?" I respond, "It was wonderful," and I'm done. But she's just warming up: "What was so wonderful about it? What happened after you left the house? Who'd you talk to on the phone? Did they talk long? How was their mood? Did they have any prayer requests? How was your lunch? Who went to lunch with you? Where did you eat? What did you eat? What else is new?" I'm out of words. I used them all up at the office! But if I'm going to be an effective communicator, I have to be willing to take a note from my wife and share the details.

Which leads right into the seventh and final step to effective communication: *listen.* The number one way to improve your relationships is by learning to really listen.

Leadership expert John C. Maxwell tells the story of an American businessman who, at an international meeting of company executives, asked an executive from Japan what he considered the most important language for world trade. The American assumed the answer would be English, but the Japanese executive smiled and said, "My customer's language."[56]

The first duty of love is to listen. You've heard the saying: "We have two ears and one mouth so that we can listen twice as much as we speak."[57] That saying is attributed to Epictetus, a Greek philosopher who was born in 50 A.D., but it doesn't take rocket science or a philosophy degree to figure it out.

Jesus's disciples were always at their best when they were sitting, listening, and learning from Jesus. It was when they opened their mouths that they got themselves into trouble. The same is true for us today. Don't listen to respond. You can't listen if you are busy planning what you're going to say next. Listen to hear. Listen to understand. Listen to love.

Take a look at this poem by Dr. Denis Waitley about the importance of listening to your children:

Take a moment to listen today
to what your children are trying to say,
Listen to them, whatever you do
or they won't be there to listen to you.

Listen to their problems, listen to their needs
Praise their smallest triumphs, praise their littlest deeds;
Tolerate their chatter, amplify their laughter,
Find out what's the matter, find out what they're after.

If we tell our children all the bad in them we see,
They'll grow up exactly how we hoped they'd never be;
But if we tell our children we're so proud to wear their name,
They'll grow up believing that they're winners in the game.

So tell them that you love them every single night;
And though you scold them make sure you hold them

*and tell them they're all right, "Good night, happy dreams,
Tomorrow's looking bright."*

*Take a moment to listen today to what
your children are trying to say.*

*Listen to them whatever you do, and
They'll be there to listen to you.*[58]

I just love that. Children spell love t-i-m-e. Take time to listen, take time to play, take time to understand, take time to love, take time to go to their recitals and ball games.

In summary: to communicate effectively, you must employ empathy, use a compassionate touch, communicate with love, allow for reaction time, pray together and for each other, share the details, and listen. If you can do all of those things, your relationships will soar on wings like eagles and not only be better than they are today, but better than you can even imagine.

TWO POWERFUL EXPRESSIONS

Let me conclude with two golden expressions in communication that you need to anchor in your mind so you'll always have them at the ready: "I'm sorry," and "I love you."

The popular 1970s film "Love Story" coined the phrase: "Love means never having to say you're sorry." That is the biggest bunch of rubbish I've ever heard. That is more fake than fake news. Romans 3:23 reminds us, "For all have sinned, and come short of the glory of God" (KJV).

We all fall short of that glorious standard, which means we'll all mess up from time to time. Your time-to-time might be measured in days or weeks or minutes or hours, depending on how honest you are. When you're wrong, say, "I'm sorry." When you're right, don't rub it in. Be quiet. ". . . and it will be well with you" (Psalm 128:2, NASB).

The second golden expression is this: "I love you." A very successful businessman came to my office in tears because his wife of fifteen years had left him. I asked him a simple question: "When was the last time you told your wife you loved her?" He had to think about it. He thought for a moment and then responded: "A few months ago, I suppose."

He thought because he'd said it once, he didn't have to say it again. He thought because he'd given her a nice house, a new car, and a credit card that would buy her however many purses and shoes she wanted, then she would be content to stay with him forever. Instead, she ran off with a man who lived in a modest home but had the one thing to give that her husband had withheld: love.

Husbands, love your wives as Christ loved the church. Wives, submit yourselves to your own husbands. This is God's divine order that brings love, joy, and peace to your marriage, making your home "as the days of heaven upon the earth" (Deuteronomy 11:21, KJV).

If you're still struggling with this chapter on communication, don't be discouraged. The words that we speak begin with the thoughts that we think. And the next chapter will help as you tap into the absolute power that God has available for you in your mind.

THE POWER OF YOUR MIND

"Our thoughts are the decorations inside the sanctuary where we live." -A.W. TOZER[59]

"Everything can be taken from a man but one thing: the last of the human freedoms–to choose one's attitude in any given set of circumstances, to choose one's own way." -VIKTOR FRANKL[60]

The human mind. What a wonder it is. What an extravagant gift from an unfathomably brilliant Creator. Listen to the voice of that Creator speak to you through His word:

*"You will keep him in perfect peace, whose mind is stayed
on you, because he trusts in you."* (Isaiah 26:3, NKJV)

*And be not conformed to this world: but be ye
transformed by the renewing of your mind, that
ye may prove what is that good, and acceptable,
and perfect, will of God.* (Romans 12:2, KJV)

*. . . and be renewed in the spirit of your mind,
and that you put on the new man which was
created according to God, in true righteousness
and holiness.* (Ephesians 4:23–24, NKJV)

*Let this mind be in you, which was also in
Christ Jesus.* (Philippians 2:5, KJV)

The message here is clear. if you want to change your
life for the better, get in control of your thought life.

Consider the story of *The Little Engine That Could.* This
story is older than I am, and I've sailed by eighty with
my hair on fire, yet children and adults the world over
will know what you are talking about when you recite the
mantra, "I think I can. I think I can. I think I can."

The story begins with train cars loaded down with
groceries and toys for little girls and boys. The problem
was, the train cars were on one side of a steep mountain

and the children were on the other. The train cars needed an engine to carry them to their destination.

Along came a shiny, new engine who could surely help without any trouble. But he was used to carrying passenger cars. He wouldn't lower himself to carry toys. Next came a big engine whose typical cargo was machines that "print books and newspapers for grown-ups to read." He thought that children's cargo was beneath him. Then a rusty, old engine came along, but he was too tired. Finally, a little blue engine approached and asked if she could help. (Interestingly, all of the engines are referred to as "he" until the little engine comes along who is identified as "she." But that's a message for another day . . .)

The little blue engine was small. She had never been over the mountain. She had never even had an official assignment. Up to this point, she had only moved cars around the railyard. But when she saw the cars and toys looking at her expectantly, "And she thought of the good little boys and girls on the other side of the mountain who would have no toys and no wholesome food unless she helped," she used the power of her mind and said: "I think I can. I think I can. I think I can." And she did![61]

The power of your mind can turn *can't* into *can* or *won't* into *will*. It can transform *impossible* into *possible* and *sorrow* into *joy*. It holds the power to covert *defeat* into *victory*, *stress* into *peace*, or *doubt* into *faith*.

I realize many cynics today roll their eyes and snort dismissively at "old fashioned" encouragements relating to positive thinking. But it's true! If you think you can . . . you will. If you think you can't . . . you won't. If you think you're beat . . . you are! If you think you'll fail . . . you will.

It's not about what you're going *through*; it's about what you're going *to*. If you're in a storm, keep rowing. If you're in a fight, fight to win. If you've been knocked down, you're not defeated unless you stay down. The Bible says that the righteous person will fall six times yet rise again (see Proverbs 24:16). Get up in Jesus's name!

On the other hand, if you drink from the toxic pools of resentment, bitterness, anger, rage, self-pity, fear, personal insecurity, and revenge, you will poison your mind. A poisoned mind will eventually destroy your physical body. But if you want to change your life for the better, you can make up your mind that you and God are going to take control of your thought life.

It's inescapable. What you permit, you promote. What you allow, you encourage. What you tolerate, you deserve. Your thought life has the power to destroy you or to lift you into the very presence of God. The choice is yours.

FEED YOUR MIND

The Bible reveals that your mind responds to what you feed it.

Before LOL or BTW or YOLO or even BFF entered our cultural vocabulary, there was GIGO. GIGO is shorthand for a principle that the early computer programmers summarized with the saying "Garbage In, Garbage Out." This described the truth that, no matter how powerful and meticulous the computer — if you input gibberish, nonsensical instructions, or poor or misinformation, then the output will be equally poor and nonsensical. You can't get good analysis out of a supercomputer that has been fed "garbage" data.

The same is true for your mind. What you put into it is what you'll get out of it. If all you watch is fake news, you'll never have a real life. If all you tell yourself is that you are a failure who will never amount to anything because you don't have the talent to screw in a lightbulb, then you will never succeed in life.

But if you pick up the Good News and read the Scriptures that tell you who God is and who God says you are, if you feast on the Word, then the result will be love, joy, patience, kindness, goodness, gentleness, self-control, and a peace that passes all understanding. Instead of Garbage In, Garbage Out, choose to put Good News In, Good News Out! Your mind responds to what you feed it.

So, what should you be feeding your mind? The apostle Paul has the secret in Philippians 4:8, passed down from generations like your great-grandmother's famous meatloaf recipe. Here it is:

Finally, brethren, whatsoever things are true, whatsoever things are honest, whatsoever things are just, whatsoever things are pure, whatsoever things are lovely, whatsoever things are of good report; if there be any virtue, and if there be any praise, think on these things. (KJV)

There you have it. If you want your meatloaf to taste just like great-grandmother's, follow her recipe exactly as it is written. And if you want to live a victorious, joyful, productive life, follow Paul's recipe for what to allow to enter into your mind.

If you grew up in poverty, abuse, neglect, in a home where there was no love or encouragement, where parents were absent or unable to care for you, I have a message for you straight from the heart of God: Today is a brand-new day.

Failure is an event, not a person. You can move past it. It is not a permanent state of being. Yesterday really did end last night and today really is a brand-new day. When God created the heavens and the earth and all that was in it, one of the first things He did was divide life into twenty-four-hour modules, separating night from day to form one day, because He knew that was all we could stand. You failed yesterday? Press on today. Not where you want to be? Keep pressing. Didn't win? Try again. Have a crappy start in life? Press on to the prize. His mercies are new every morning.

You must understand that you are what you are and where you are because of what is in your mind. When you change your thinking, you change your actions; when you change your actions, you change your future. The question is: What are you putting in your mind?

Stop watching eight hours of toxic television a day. When you turn off fake news and pick up the Good News, you feed your mind on higher things.

Feed your mind on the joy of the Lord that makes rich and adds no sorrow. Joy is powerful. The pain of the past is forgotten. Joy is where heaven comes down and glory fills your soul.

Feed your mind on the love of God that loved you so much He gave His only begotten Son that you might become sons and daughters of the King of glory! You are royalty. Your past is forgiven and forgotten. God your Father has taken your poverty and given you the royal robe of righteousness and the riches of Abraham — you are a rags-to-riches success story! Rejoice and be exceedingly glad!

Feed your mind on the faith that we have in the Living God. Faith is the victory that overcomes the world. Faith opens the storehouses of heaven for every blessing God has stored up for you. Faith starts out before you know how it's going to turn out. Faith moves mountains of impossibility. Faith releases the healing power of God to restore your health, your marriage, your family, and your finances. Faith is the substance of things hoped for, the evidence of things not seen (see Hebrews 11:1).

IT'S YOUR CHOICE

Let me be straight with you for a moment. You are the way you are because that's the way you want to be. Before you start to object, before the word "but" comes out of your mouth, let me stop you right there. Because the truth of the matter is, if you really wanted to be different, you would be in the process of changing right now.

The apostle Paul said this:

Not that I have already attained, or am already perfected; but I press on, that I may lay hold of that for which Christ Jesus has also laid hold of me. Brethren, I do not count myself to have apprehended; but one thing I do, forgetting those things which are behind and reaching forward to those things which are ahead, I press toward the goal for the prize of the upward call of God in Christ Jesus. Therefore let us, as many as are mature, have this mind; and if in anything you think otherwise, God will reveal even this to you. Nevertheless, to the degree that we have already attained, let us walk by the same rule, let us be of the same mind. (Philippians 3:12–16, NKJV)

Paul, who was beaten, shipwrecked, stoned and left for dead, bitten by a deadly viper, and put into Roman prisons said, in essence, "I haven't learned all that I should yet, but I keep working toward the day when I will finally be all that Christ saved me for and wants me to be. I'm still working toward the day when: all my thoughts are His thoughts; all my words are His words; all my actions are His actions; all my love is His love; all my joy is His joy." That's Paul. Clearly, you and I should never stop trying to be better than we are.

What is the focus of your thoughts? What is the content of your self-talk or internal dialogue? What battle rages right now in your mind? Keep fighting, keep pressing, keep working until you are of the same mind as Christ.

OLD DOGS, NEW TRICKS

No matter how old you are, you are younger today than you'll ever be again. The logic of that statement is inescapable!

"Old" is when your friends compliment you on your new alligator shoes and you're actually barefoot. Old is when a beautiful woman catches your eye and your pacemaker opens the garage door. Old is when two ninety-year-old people get married and spend their honeymoon trying to get out of the car.

Stop looking for a place to quit; you're only sixty! Moses died at one hundred and twenty, and he walked to his own funeral. In the words of the poet Robert Frost, you've got "miles to go before you sleep."[62] You can rest when you're dead!

I once read that you have not truly become old until you allow regrets to replace your dreams. King David said, "Even when I am old and gray, do not forsake me, my God, till I declare your power to the next generation, your mighty acts to all who are to come" (Psalm 71:18, NIV). This is God's message to his grey-headed legions: finish strong! Fight the good fight until your last day and last breath.

Fact: The way you see yourself will affect your performance today and tomorrow.

Nothing will ever be attempted if all possible objections must first be overcome. Dr. Luke recorded these words from the mouth of Jesus: "The things which are impossible with men are possible with God" (Luke 18:27, KJV).

Fact: Everything is impossible until someone does it.

Men couldn't fly for centuries until the Wright Brothers completed the first flight in an engine-powered aircraft in 1903 at Kitty Hawk, North Carolina. Then suddenly everyone was creating "flying machines" and before you knew it, we had a man on the moon! The Wright Brothers didn't break the sound barrier; they did something even more important. They broke the thought barrier that said it couldn't be done.

The horseless carriage was impossible until Henry Ford created it.

The idea that frozen food could actually taste good was impossible until Clarence Birdseye spent time in the Artic watching the Inuit Indians "quick freeze" the fish they caught.[63] The global frozen food market is now valued at over 290 billion USD.[64]

Nationwide overnight delivery wasn't feasible, according to Fred Smith's economics professor at Yale University, who gave Smith a "C" grade on the term paper that laid out such a concept. Smith's company, FedEx, began operation in April 1971 and now delivers more than six million packages each working day.[65]

All of the spiritual advisors available to me at age twenty-six told me that building a non-denominational Evangelical Church in San Antonio, Texas, with five thousand seats and filling them all every Sunday morning wasn't possible. But with God's help, we did it! On dedication Sunday, six thousand were in attendance. Nothing is impossible with God; NOTHING!

Luke 1:37 says, "For with God nothing will be impossible" (NKJV). John 14:13 says, "And whatever you ask in my name, that I will do" (NKJV). Put those two promises of God together and you have a blank check to be what you want to be, go where you want to go, and do what you want to do — because no one can defeat you!

Nothing is impossible with God!

AND . . . ACTION!

Passivity, lethargy, or paralysis never accomplished anything worthwhile.

God's message to the Church through Peter was, "Therefore, prepare your minds for action, keep sober in spirit, fix your hope completely on the grace to be brought to you at the revelation of Jesus Christ" (1 Peter 1:13, NASB).

"Prepare your minds for action." Action is the foundation key to all success. The Church was established by action. Jesus gave the twelve disciples a command called "the great commission." That command was: "Go into all the world and preach the gospel" (Mark 16:15, NKJV). He didn't say, ". . . form a committee and talk an idea to death." He said, "Go." He said, "Preach."

He didn't say, "Look for twelve people who will agree with you." He didn't tell them to wait until the printing press is invented. He didn't say wait until the radio comes along, or until a color TV is in every household in America. He didn't say wait until you can read the Bible on your smart phone or live Tweet your way across the Holy Land.

He said a right-now message: "Go. Go with the message I have given you. Go in the power of My name. Go heal the sick. Go cast out demons. Go with the power of the Word. Go with the anointing of the Holy Spirit. Go!"

One of my favorite quotations of all time is this one by President Calvin Coolidge:

Nothing in this world can take the place of persistence. Talent will not; nothing is more common than unsuccessful men with talent. Genius will not; unrewarded genius is almost a proverb. Education will not; the world is full of educated derelicts. Persistence and determination alone are omnipotent. The slogan Press On! has solved and always will solve the problems of the human race.[66]

Press on! Be better. Think better. Live better. Prepare you mind for action and go!

ATTITUDE IS EVERYTHING

I checked my luggage at the airport in Washington D.C. recently when I noticed mistletoe tied above the luggage rack. I asked what it was for and I was told, "That's so you can kiss your luggage goodbye."

In a church in the Deep South, the pastor was late for Sunday morning service when suddenly the devil appeared in the pulpit. Church members dove out the windows and ran out the doors screaming in terror. However, a man on the front row didn't move, didn't even blink an eye. The devil asked, "Aren't you afraid of me?" The man said, "Absolutely not!" The devil replied, "Why not?" and the man said, "Because for the past twenty years I've been living with your sister!"

Your attitude is a direct reflection of your thought life. Your thought life is the "advance man" of your true self. Its roots are hidden but its fruit is visible. How would you like it if your husband or wife could read your thoughts? How about your boss? What if I told you that I can tell exactly what you've been thinking about by listening to you talk? The roots may be hidden, but the fruit is the evidence. As the poem goes, "For sinew and blood are a thin veil of lace; what you wear in your heart you wear on your face!"[67]

Compare and contrast the mental attitudes of Thomas and Paul.

Thomas had Jesus, the Son of God, for a pastor. He personally witnessed Jesus performing miracles for three-and-a-half years. Yet he could not believe that Christ had resurrected unless he saw Jesus's nail-scarred hands for himself.

Paul, on the other hand, was beaten, stoned, shipwrecked, imprisoned, betrayed, and left for dead, yet said, "our light and momentary troubles are achieving for us an eternal glory that far outweighs them all" (2 Corinthians 4:17, NIV).

Is your attitude more like doubting Thomas, or the apostle Paul?

Stop saying, "I can't," and start saying, "I *can* do all things through Christ." Stop saying, "If . . .", and start saying, "I *will* by God's grace." Stop saying, "It's impossible," and start saying, "*Nothing is impossible* to those that believe. He has all power in heaven and earth!"

Stop saying "I don't know the right people," and get to know the Father, Son, and Holy Ghost. Quit saying "I'm not educated." James wrote, "If any of you lacks wisdom, let him ask God, who gives generously to all without reproach, and it will be given him" (James 1:5, ESV). Jesus chose fishermen to be His closest friends, who were described as "unschooled, ordinary men" (Acts 4:13, NIV). Their wisdom and power didn't come from books or a college education, it came from Jesus and it came from the Father who lavishes on all who ask for it.

Replace, "I'm too old," with "Moses was still ministering at 120." Replace, "I'm too young," with Paul's words to Timothy: "Don't let anyone think less of you because you are young. Be an example to all believers in what you say, in the way you live, in your love, your faith, and your purity" (1 Timothy 4:12, NLT).

Surround yourself with people whose lives are happy and fulfilled and you will be surrounded with people whose speech is peppered with praise. People who lead unhappy, unfulfilled lives, who are constantly whining about their job, their spouse, their health, their preacher, are not the kinds of friends who will make you better. They will only make you bitter.

You need a friend like James, and I'm not talking about James Taylor. The Bible says, "Count it all joy, my brothers, when you meet trials of various kinds" (James 1:2, ESV). Count it ALL. Everything that happens to you is an opportunity for joy with the right perspective and the right mental attitude. If you get up from reading this and stub your toe, I want you to shout, "1, 2, 3 . . . I'm counting until I get to joy. Hallelujah!"

Let me teach you a therapeutic phrase that can turn your life around. It's so simple, yet it really works. Are you ready? The phrase is, "GET OVER IT!" Thinking about every miserable experience you've had for the past ten years? Get over it. Have you been hurt and fearful that you are going to get hurt again? Get over it. Have you been criticized? Get over it. Have you been rejected? Get over it. Have you been betrayed? Get over it. Have you failed? Get over it. Get over it. Get over it. This is a new day. Act like it. Talk like it. Think like it.

It would be impossible to estimate the number of jobs lost, marriages ruined, promotions missed, sales not made, because of someone's inability to get over it, get up, and keep moving forward. Whatever is holding you back today, take that thought captive and say, "I'M OVER IT!"

THE DAY OF ADVERSITY

Adversity comes to all of us. Jesus said, "In the world ye shall have tribulation." (John 16:33, KJV). And you will. There's no getting around it. I'm sorry to say it but that is one of the promises of God and it's for you. You will have trouble. But the brightest crowns in heaven have been polished and glorified through the furnace of tribulation and adversity. They are made of gold that has been tried by fire.

Adversity does not make a person either weak or strong, but adversity reveals what you are. Proverbs 24:10 says, "If you faint in the day of adversity, your strength is small" (ESV). Paul wrote to the Corinthian church, "my strength is made perfect in weakness" (2 Corinthians 12:9, KJV). How is that possible? Because it's not in yours and my strength, it's in God's. You can see more on your knees in prayer than you can see through a telescope from the Eiffel Tower.

Deuteronomy 33:25 says, "As your days, so shall your strength be" (NKJV). That means that up to the last day and the last hour you live, you can do good things through the power of God. God's strength will be with you for all the days of your life. Have you ever been around someone who was on their deathbed, and then suddenly, miraculously, for a moment or a day they were reinvigorated and able to have a final meal, final conversation, final hug before crossing over? That is the kind of strength we are talking about here. The kind of strength that can only come from God. The kind of strength that shows up when you have nothing left to give.

Scripture is full of reminders that God is our refuge and strength (Psalm 46:1), the strength of our lives (Psalm 27:1), our rock and fortress and deliverer (Psalm 18:2), our high tower (Psalm 144:2), our shelter in the storm, our shield in the day of battle, the rock of our salvation. He is the greatest, the wisest, the highest.

Our God is the God of Abraham, Isaac, and Jacob. He is your Provider, the Light in the darkness, protection against powers and principalities. His eye is on the sparrow and His eye is on you. Can you feel your spirits lifting by adding those thoughts to your mind? Isaiah 40:31 says, "But they that wait upon the LORD shall renew their strength; they shall mount up with wings as eagles; they shall run, and not be weary; and they shall walk, and not faint" (KJV).

Satan attacks anything God has chosen to promote. Is your thought life under fire? Your promotion is coming! Michael English sings in one of his songs, "There is not a victory without a fight. There is not a sunrise without a night. There is not a purchase without a cost. There is not a crown without a cross."[68]

THE MIND OF CHRIST

A small clothing store was threatened with extinction by a national chain store that bought all the property on the block surrounding the small business. However, the owner refused to sell. More importantly, he refused to be intimidated. The large corporation threatened to build around him and put him out of business, but the small business owner stood firm. True to its threat, the chain store built a massive store that surrounded the small merchant on three sides. Signs were posted everywhere, "Grand Opening!" The little merchant countered with a banner of his own, stretching across the entire width of his store: "Main Entrance."

Philippians 2:5 says, "Let this mind be in you, which was also in Christ Jesus" (KJV). The mind of Christ knows there is nothing to fear with God on your side.

The mind of Christ knows that with God all things are possible. The mind of Christ knows that beauty comes from ashes.

Consider David and Goliath. When the giant Philistine named Goliath came up against the Israelites, the Israelite soldiers all thought he was so big they could never kill him. David looked at the same giant and thought, "He's so big, I can't miss him!" Same problem, different mind.

Two shoe salesmen were sent to an island to sell shoes. Upon arrival, the first salesman was shocked to realize that no one wore shoes. Immediately he sent a telegram to his home office that said, "Will return home tomorrow. No one here wears shoes." The second salesman was sent to the same island. He also sent a telegram immediately home, yet his telegram said, "Please send me every pair of shoes you have in the warehouse . . . everyone here needs shoes!" Same problem, different mindset.

You can have the mind of Christ simply by filling your thoughts with what God says about you. One of the most powerful verses in the Word of God comes from the prophet Isaiah:

> *"The Spirit of the LORD God is upon Me, because the Lord has anointed Me to preach good tidings to the poor; He has sent Me to heal the brokenhearted, to proclaim liberty to the captives, and the opening of the prison to those who are bound; to proclaim*

the acceptable year of the LORD, and the day of
vengeance of our God; to comfort all who mourn, to
console those who mourn in Zion, to give them beauty
for ashes, the oil of joy for mourning, the garment
of praise for the spirit of heaviness; that they may be
called trees of righteousness, the planting of the LORD,
that He may be glorified." (Isaiah 61:1–3, NKJV)

There is power in these words, power that is yours when you sear these verses into your mind. Jesus came so that you would be healthy and whole. Jesus came to break the chains that bind you. Comfort is yours. Joy is yours. Beauty is made out of the ashes of your pain and your past. Praise covers your depression. Victory is yours. Peace that passes understanding is yours. The oil of joy has been brought to your marriage. Your family will be reunited. Your finances will be restored. Everything that is broken will heal. You are royalty. You are righteous. God is glorified through your life.

Ephesians 2:10 says, "For we are God's handiwork, created in Christ Jesus to do good works, which God prepared in advance for us to do" (NIV). No one can make you feel inferior without your consent. You are a divine original. No one on the earth is quite like you. There are 7.8 billion people on the earth and not one of them has the same fingerprints or the exact same DNA as you. If they did, you could get away with murder.

God has all kinds of measures in place to keep you on the straight and narrow, and to show you how special you are. He knows the structure of your DNA, so don't offend Him by trying to be a cheap copy of somebody else. Be who you are. Be glad to be who you are. Because who you are is a child of God, created on purpose for a purpose, by your Father in heaven. What is on God's mind? YOU! You are on the very mind of Christ. Think about that!

A MULE AND A MAESTRO

A Missouri mule fell into a deep pit. He was owned by a cruel farmer who thought the mule was too old and that it would cost too much to dig him out. So the farmer decided to bury him. He began to throw trash down into that deep pit on top of his faithful mule. The mule shook his whole body every time a shovel full fell on him. He shook it off, stomped on the trash, and stood tall on the trash he had packed down.

Day after day, shovel full of trash after shovel full of trash, the Missouri mule with an attitude of fortitude shook it off, stomped on the trash, and stood tall. One day the cruel farmer threw one load of trash too many onto the faithful mule. The mule shook it off, stomped it down, and jumped right out of that pit and ran to his freedom.

My friend, sooner or later, someone will throw their trash on you. Shake it off! Stomp on it. Use that trash for an elevator to reach for the stars. County it all joy! Press on. Persistence overcomes resistance. As a man thinketh so is he!

Let me close this chapter with a true story. A mother had given her nine-year-old son piano lessons. It was clear that he was going nowhere fast; a maestro in the making he was not. In desperation, the mother bought two tickets for her son and herself to hear the great Polish pianist, Paderewski, in concert.

When they arrived at the concert hall, the mother became engrossed in conversation with the woman sitting next to her. Meanwhile, her nine-year-old son saw the massive ebony Steinway grand piano and walked right up on stage and started playing Chopsticks.

The crowd was horrified. They all shouted for the boy to stop and exit the stage. But the great Paderewski, hearing the commotion, walked out on stage and told the boy, "Don't quit." Paderewski sat down beside the boy and started playing a masterful, improvised composition built simply to the tune the boy was playing. The crowd exploded with applause.[69]

Sometimes in life your best sounds like "Chopsticks." But suddenly, God shows up and says, "Don't quit." The Master's concerto makes our meager efforts beautiful, and the world is amazed.

Are things going wrong for you? Keep playing! Keep trying. The Master is coming to make your life beautiful. Fix your mind on that!

−SEVEN−

THE POWER OF TWO

Two people are better off than one, for they can help each other succeed. If one person falls, the other can reach out and help. But someone who falls alone is in real trouble. Likewise, two people lying close together can keep each other warm. But how can one be warm alone? A person standing alone can be attacked and defeated, but two can stand back-to-back and conquer. Three are even better, for a triple-braided cord is not easily broken. (ECCLESIASTES 4:9-12, NLT)

"Two heads are better than one, not because either is infallible, but because they are unlikely to go wrong in the same direction." -C.S. LEWIS[70]

The Bible is a book of numbers. One is the number of unity. Two is the power of two. Three is the number of the Trinity: God the Father, God the Son, God the Holy Spirit. Four is the number of the earth. Six is the number of sin. Seven is the number of perfection and completion. Eight is the number of new beginnings. Twelve is the number of government. Eighteen is the number of life. The numerology of the Bible goes on and on. This is a book of very sophisticated mathematics with a message that is very clear in both language and numbers.

The Bible says no man can serve two masters. If you're looking for a verse that will prove polygamy won't work, that's it.

There are two positions in Scripture: you are either saved or you're lost; you're either wheat or tares; you're a sheep or a goat; you're on your way to heaven or hell; you're on the broad way that leads to the gates of hell or the narrow way that leads to heaven; you represent the kingdom of light or the kingdom of darkness.

You can't be "sort of" saved any more than you can "sort of" shoot a shotgun or "sort of" be pregnant; you are or you're not! You are either a servant of Jesus Christ or a slave to sin and Satan. It's that simple! I've heard people say they are "sort of" saved. No, you're not! You have either received Jesus Christ as your Lord and Savior, or you haven't!

The Word is a two-edged sword. It divides light from darkness. It divides the bone from the marrow. It divides the intent of a man's heart. That means, through the power of the Holy Bible, you can know the motive of a man's heart when he speaks. It divides fear from faith. Fear says you're defeated; faith leaps back and says greater is He that is in you than he that is in the world (see 1 John 4:4). Fear says you're alone; faith says, "I will never leave you nor forsake you even to the ends of the earth."

Fear says you're financially ruined; faith leaps back and says it is the Lord who gives you power to get wealth. He will give you houses you did not build, wells you did not dig, vineyards you did not plant. He shall plant you like a tree by streams of living water, and whatsoever you do shall prosper. Fear tells you your sickness is fatal. Faith on the other hand leaps on the stage of your thoughts and says you shall live and not die; by His stripes you are healed. Jesus is the same yesterday, today, and forever. What He did by the Sea of Galilee, He can do right where you are today.

Jesus sent out His disciples two-by-two. He didn't send them out a dozen at a time with a million-dollar budget and a public address system. Their simple method of evangelism was to go, knock on the door, and extend peace upon each house. Jesus instructed them: if they returned that peace, then you found someone you could witness to; if they started giving you a lot of lip, shake the dust off your feet and leave. It would be better for Sodom and Gomorrah than to waste your time with those people.

There are two wills of God. There is the sovereign will of God, which says that there are things that are going to happen whether you want them to happen or not. For instance, in the Book of Genesis, God established in His sovereign will that the Jewish people were going to be the heirs of a special land grant that in time would be called Israel. It makes no difference what the United Nations wants. It doesn't make any difference what Iran wants, what China or Russia wants. God is going to see to it that the Jewish people have the land of Israel. They are not interlopers; they own that land! (Genesis 17:7–8)

That sovereign will, in the Greek, is the *beulemah* of God. But there is also the *philemah* of God, that is the "wish" or desire of God. The Bible says it is the wish of God that all men come to repentance (see 2 Peter 3:9). Obviously not all men are coming to repentance; that's why there's a hell.

There are preachers in America teaching that everyone is already saved, some just don't know it yet. That is not true at all. If you have not confessed and forsaken your sin and received Jesus Christ as Lord, you have not come to salvation. Jesus Christ is the answer. You must come to Him and accept Him as your substitutionary sacrifice at the cross; only then are you purchased at the price of His blood. That is salvation.

Jesus told the parable of the two builders who built two houses upon two different foundations (see Matthew 7:24–27). The one built his house upon the rock. (He read the Word; he heard the Word; he lived the Word. It was the rock upon which his house, his faith, was built.) The other built his house upon the sand. He was a disciple of hot tub Christianity. The wind was in his hair and he could sit on his front porch and dip his toes in the sea. (He knew the Word, too, but he never obeyed the Word.) "It is better to obey than to sacrifice." (1 Samuel 15:22).

The man who built his house upon the rock was sweating as he watched the other man drink iced tea and dangle his toes in the surf. The house built upon the rock appeared to be built upon struggle, while the house built upon the sand appeared to be built on ease.

The storms of life are a promise. Jesus said, "And when the storm comes . . . " So along came a storm, and guess what happened? The winds blew and the waves crashed, and one house stood firm while the other was decimated into floating debris as far as the eye could see. One house — the shifting-sand, go-with-the-flow, follow the fads of life and promises of instant success — was torn apart. The other house — built upon the rock, produced through struggle and endurance, followed by unlimited success — stood firm. Which house are you building?

TWO ARE BETTER THAN ONE

Solomon, the wisest man in the Bible, wrote these words in Ecclesiastes 4:9: "Two are better than one, because they have a good reward for their labor" (NKJV).

I always think of that verse when I see a man wearing suspenders and a belt. Why do you need both? I suppose because two are better than one.

Two are better than one. Remember that when you look at your wife. God said it is not good for man to be alone. A man needs a helpmate — to help meet the boat note, help meet the car note, help meet the house note, and all the other notes.

In God's math, His supernatural factor kicks in whenever there are two. There is something called a "quantum leap" in mathematics. God has a quantum leap that runs off the page. The Bible says one can chase a thousand; then it says two can put ten thousand to flight (see Deuteronomy 32:30). If one can chase a thousand, logic would say that two can chase two-thousand, but God says two can chase ten thousand because they have a supernatural power that goes into overdrive — a quantum leap beyond your wildest imagination.

Can you imagine what would happen in America if millions of evangelicals started praying in unity in the authority of God's Word, in the authority of Jesus's name? It would set this country on fire. Let's do it! In Jesus's name. Starting with two.

Listen closely. This may be the most important point in this whole chapter. *Dominion over every problem that you have begins with two in agreement in Jesus's name.* In your finances, in your health, in your relationships, in your emotions, in your marriage, with your children, in a business crisis — two in agreement can do more than two million in disagreement.

Jesus said in Matthew 18, "Again I say to you that if two of you agree on earth concerning anything that they ask, it will be done for them by My Father in heaven. For where two or three are gathered together in My name, I am there in the midst of them" (Matthew 18:19–20, NKJV).

Look at these twosomes in the Bible.

Joshua and Caleb whipped the giants that two million said, "we cannot handle!" Who were the two people who entered the Promised Land? Joshua and Caleb. Why? Because they were two in agreement, so God gave them the power to do what they professed in faith they could do.

Paul and Silas sang in prison and the jailhouse shook — the first jailhouse rock! The earth quaked and they walked out with the keys in one hand and a convert in the other because of the power of two.

Peter and John were headed into the temple when they saw a man who had been lame since he was in his mother's womb. When the man asked for alms, John didn't say, "We have a committee for the handicapped at our church." What Peter said was, "I have no silver and gold, but what I do have I give to you. In the name of Jesus of Nazareth, rise up and walk!" (Acts 3:6, ESV). What I do have is the power of two. What I do have is a solution for your need. What I do have is worth more than silver and gold. What I do have is far greater than you can imagine. Christ is the answer!

There are two witnesses in the Book of Revelation (see Revelation 11:3). Those two witnesses are Enoch and Elijah, two Old Testament prophets who were taken to heaven yet did not die. Listen to the power God is going to give these two men: they are going to have power to turn water to blood; they are going to have power to call fire from heaven; they are going to have power to call plagues and drought to cover the earth. Elijah will have fire-breathing power that will incinerate anyone who tries to hurt him. Talk about crowd control!

Mary and Joseph, two in agreement. When Herod started slaughtering the infants in Bethlehem, Mary and Joseph did not attack each other. Mary didn't blame Joseph for her birth plan falling apart. She didn't criticize him for taking her to a barn instead of to a hospital. They were a united front. When the Pharisees denounced their son as a heretic and a demonized teacher, when Rome called Him a traitor, Mary and Joseph stood together because the power of two parents in agreement crushes the Roman Empire.

Satan's first attack was on a husband and a wife in the Garden of Eden. Satan knew that if he could divide them, he could destroy them. And he did divide them, and he did destroy them. They ate the forbidden fruit and we've been working from daylight to dark ever since because they ate us out of house and home.

Now ask yourself, "How can a person experience the power of two if married to an unbeliever?" The answer is, "They cannot." If you're dating an unbeliever, tell him or her goodbye; do it now!

SUPERNATURAL ENEMIES

Why is the supernatural power of two vitally important? Because you have supernatural enemies.

Ephesians 6:12 says, "For we wrestle not against flesh and blood, but against principalities, against powers, against the rulers of the darkness of this world, against spiritual wickedness in high places" (KJV). This verse is speaking of Satan and his angels and his demonic agents. Your enemies are supernatural. They are organized into rank just like the military. They have a geographical area to cover, hence the Prince of Persia (see Daniel 10:20).

They are totally committed to your destruction. Satan is very real. He is your sworn enemy. The Bible says he has come to rob, to kill, and to destroy (see John 10:10). Satan is the father of lies. He's a divider. If he can divide the husband and wife, he can destroy the family. If he can divide the father and son, and the mothers and daughters, he'll destroy the next generation. If he can pit race against race, he can divide the nation. If he can divide the nations, he can create continual war.

If he can divide the Church, he can make it weak and sickly and appear to the world to be a congregation of foolish people who know how to do nothing. Satan is a roaring lion. He's the father of fear. And he's trying to destroy you, your children, your marriage, your business, your health, and your dreams any way he can.

I vividly recall the young mother who came to me with a ten-year-old daughter who had suddenly become controlled by fear. The daughter had become obsessed with the thought of death. I talked to the daughter briefly and then I asked the mother, "What are you allowing your daughter to watch on television?" She told me, and I said, "Don't you know those shows are rooted in the occult? You are letting people into your house to program your child's mind with fear and death. This child is being totally driven by that."

Know what your children are watching. It's possible you are allowing people into your house through your television who you wouldn't allow to cross your threshold even if you had a shotgun in your hand. Watch what your children are watching! Sexual predators are surfing the Web searching for their next victim.

Over a century ago, before television was invented, a Danish philosopher and scientist, Soren Kierkegaard, wrote: "Suppose someone invented an instrument, a convenient little talking tube, which could be heard over the whole land. I wonder if the police would forbid it, fearing that the whole country would become mentally deranged if it were used."[71] Brother, was he ever on target!

Studies show that over 500,000 children in America are taking some form of anti-psychotic drug — including tens of thousands of preschoolers.[72] Why? In large part because of what they're watching on television or the internet.

Instead of letting your child spend four hours staring at a screen after school every day, what if you spent even a quarter of that time having a real conversation with them, warning them about the real dangers out there rather than letting them fill their mind with demonic forces? A conversation that could be had in an American home right now is beware of the drug pusher in the park; be careful who you're talking to on video games, it might be a sex trafficker; beware of guns and knives and gangs at school.

With all the mass shootings and suicide bombers in the news, it's time for America's parents to reconnect with their children, because God gave you those children to raise in the fear and the admonition of the Lord, not to serve them to the devil on a silver platter while they're in your home.

The devil is real and it's time to kick him out of our homes and the Church. We are in a spiritual war: get in it!

TO BIND AND TO LOOSE

Jesus said in Luke 11, "When a strong man, fully armed, guards his own house, his possessions are safe. But when someone stronger attacks and overpowers him, he takes away the armor in which the man trusted and divides up his plunder" (vv. 21–22, NIV). In Matthew 12:29, Jesus said, "Or how can one enter a strong man's house and plunder his goods, unless he first binds the strong man? And then he will plunder his house" (NKJV).

There is a strongman — I'm obviously talking about Satan — whose objective is to attack you, your marriage, your health, your home, your finances, your children, and your peace with the intent to utterly destroy you. How do you defeat him? Bind him.

It takes two in agreement to take dominion. Jesus said in Matthew 16:19, "And I will give you the keys of the kingdom of heaven, and whatever you bind on earth will be bound in heaven, and whatever you loose on earth will be loosed in heaven" (NKJV). You have the keys to the kingdom. You have the power to do two things: to bind or to loose on earth. When you exercise that power, you partner with God and He does the mirror copy of that action in heaven. So when you bind the strongman — the devil — on earth, God binds him in heaven. Don't let the devil's army loose in your life. Bind him in Jesus's name!

That means if a strongman — a spiritual power or force — enters your house and tries to attack your marriage, your health, your finances, your children, you take the Word of God and the blood of the Cross and the authority of Jesus's name and you bind him. It's like taking ropes of steel and wrapping them around him until he cannot breathe.

You have bound him until he's totally helpless and harmless to stop you from fulfilling the destiny God has given you to do. All you have to do is mention the name of Jesus. You have power; use it! You have authority; use it! You have dominion; use it! In your finances, in your health, in your emotions, with your children, do not let fear, depression, bitterness, or resentment drive you. Bind it. Kick it out of your house in Jesus's name. He's the Lord of your life; act like it!

Isaiah 45:11 says, "command ye me" (KJV). God is saying to men: "Tell Me what you want Me to do for you." There are people right now reading this who are waiting for God to do something. But God is saying, "I am not going to do anything until you bind something on earth, then I will bind it in heaven. When you loose something on earth, I will loose it in heaven. The action comes from earth first. 'Command ye Me' and when you speak in Jesus's name, I will do it."

You have not, because you ask not. Stand up! Speak up, church of Jesus Christ. The power is available; turn it loose!

TWO SONS

The story of the prodigal son begins, "There was a man who had two sons . . ." (Luke 15:11, ESV). This is a story of love and hate, lust and greed, rebellion and repentance, envy and jealousy, forgiveness and redemption. The total Gospel story is in this story of the lost boy. But there isn't just one son in the story; there are two.

The story actually begins, as Jesus tells it, in the first verses of chapter fifteen of the Gospel of Luke:

> *Then all the tax collectors and the sinners drew near to Him to hear Him. And the Pharisees and scribes complained, saying, "This Man receives sinners and eats with them." So He spoke this parable to them, saying: . . .* (Luke 15:1–3, NKJV)

Here Jesus eats with publicans and prostitutes. Get that picture in your mind. This is not a story you hear every day in church. Jesus, the Son of God, the very essence of purity, holy and sinless, is eating with them, which in the Bible is a sign of covenant. How do you reconcile those two things? The Pharisees looked at Jesus and said, "He calls himself the Son of God, but He's eating with sinners — the worst of the worst!" (see Mark 2:16).

Fast forward to the twenty-first century. Imagine I'm hosting a lunch for prostitutes in downtown San Antonio. What would people do? They would call the local newspaper and say, "He's lost his mind!"

There's a powerful message for the church here. The church in America is as guilty as the Pharisees who separated, divided, and categorized people. The Church rejects and resents people based on such things as the clothes they wear, the cars they drive, what neighborhood they live in, what level of education they may or may not have, the color of their skin, even, heaven help us, what denomination they belong to.

I was raised in a denomination that felt like we were going to have a subdivision in heaven with a security gate on it! Now there are 300 denominations squabbling over the Gospel. If we would fight the devil as hard as we fight each other, the devil would be in the back alleys of hell sucking on a Maalox bottle right now!

The prostitute, the drug addict, someone with a criminal past — too many churchgoers will tell them they have no place in the body of Christ. I want to tell you, one of the best friends I have ever had is a man who spent eight years in a penitentiary. He was a preacher's boy. He got saved and became hilariously wealthy in the construction business.

When I came through Dallas to go to North Texas University and was about to starve to death, that man gave me a job, a good job; and it made my graduate experience a thing of joy instead of agony. Don't ever write somebody off because of their past. Don't you allow somebody else to say your past controls your future. If you have asked Jesus Christ to forgive you of your past, you are as free as you can be: "So if the Son sets you free, you will be free indeed" (John 8:36, NIV).

- The church is not here to see who we can reject; the church is here to see who we can restore.
- The church is not here to see who we can turn away; the church is here to see who we can bring in.
- The church is not here to see who we can put down; the church is here to see who we can pick up.
- The church is not here to condemn and to criticize; the church is here to see who we can heal, restore, and convert to Jesus Christ, the Light of the World.

Please take note: "And the Spirit and the bride say, Come. And let him that heareth say, Come. And let him that is athirst come. AND WHOSOEVER WILL, let him take the water of life freely" (Revelation 22:17, KJV, emphasis added). "Whosever will," let him come. The up and the out, the down and the out, the intellectual and the illiterate, the powerful, the poor, from the guttermost to the uttermost: Jesus can save them all!

Now, back to the prodigal son. I love this kid. On the other hand, I'd like to slap his jaws till his head spins like a top. He's a hormone hurricane looking for a place to happen. He's the picture of arrogance. He's cocky. He's a rebel without a cause. He says to his father, "Father, give me the share of property that is coming to me" (Luke 15:12, ESV). It was arrogant because his father was not yet dead. It was arrogant because by the law of Moses, his older brother was going to get two-thirds of it.

I saw a sign the other day that said, "Attention teenagers. Are you tired of being harassed by your old-fashioned parents? Act now! Move out! Get a job! Pay your bills while you still know everything." Well, the prodigal son fell for that invitation.

The absolute essence of the word "prodigal" is "recklessly extravagant." If you allow your child to live in reckless extravagance, you will raise a prodigal son or daughter every time. You can't give your child too much love, but you can give your child too many things. I've heard parents say, "I want to give my son or daughter what I didn't get." The problem is you're so busy giving them what you didn't get, you don't give them what you did get — a fundamental knowledge of responsibility. If I had said to my German daddy, "give me," that's as far as I would have gotten. The next voice I would have heard would have been the voice of Saint Peter in heaven saying, "Welcome home, stupid boy!"

Notice the fine points of this story. The story starts with the son going to his father saying, "Give me." The story ends with him coming home to his father saying, "Make me." The story begins with him leaving home a son and ends with him coming home begging to be a slave. The story begins with him getting what he wanted but losing what he had. He took freedom and destroyed himself with it.

Freedom is not the right to do as you want. Freedom is shouldering the responsibility to do as you ought.

Winston Churchill once said, "The price of greatness is responsibility."[73] One of the great moral defects of our country right now is that no one wants to take responsibility for their actions. From the White House to the courthouse, we've got to learn how to take responsibility for who we are, what we say, and what we do.

So, this arrogant, smart aleck kid took all his wit and wisdom and landed in a muddy stinking hog pen, fighting slimy squealing hogs for enough slop to eat to keep from starving to death. When you're telling that story to a group of Jewish people who are not even supposed to touch pork, they recognize it's the lowest of the low. If fish food is brain food this kid needs to eat a whale. A Jewish boy, feeding with pigs, on a pagan's farm. That's the absolute bottom. But that is where every child goes who rebels against the spiritual authority of a loving and godly father.

Noah was the spiritual authority of Ham. When Ham criticized his father, God cursed Ham for it, and did so generationally. Be careful when you start criticizing spiritual authority. God will take it up with you in a very serious way.

Absalom mocked his father David. And Absalom died hanging from a tree by his hair, as spears were thrown at his chest by the reigning general in David's army, because he defied his father's authority.

Young people, if you are looking at your father on this earth and you're screaming, "Give me," and you've become a silent rebel to his authority, be very careful because God in heaven is watching you. You're tottering on the edge of using your freedom to destroy yourself. Freedom is a package deal. It comes with responsibility, and responsibility has consequences. Your choices have consequences. The far country is not a place; it's a condition of the heart, a condition of the heart that says I can live without God; I can live without spiritual authority. Listen to me: NO, YOU CAN'T!

The Bible says it this way:

*Whoever remains stiff-necked after many rebukes will suddenly be destroyed —
without remedy.* (Proverbs 29:1, NIV)

The soul that sinneth, it shall die. (Ezekiel 18:20, KJV)

For the wages of sin is death; but the gift of God is eternal life through Jesus Christ our Lord. (Romans 6:23, KJV)

Get up and get out of that hog pen thinking that says you don't need to obey spiritual authority. The sooner you do, the more blessed you're going to be.

Look at the prodigal's conclusion. He's in this hog pen, fighting for food, and he says, ". . . 'How many of my father's hired servants have bread enough to spare, and I perish with hunger! I will arise and go to my father, and will say to him, "Father, I have sinned against heaven and before you, and I am no longer worthy to be called your son. Make me like one of your hired servants"'" (Luke 15:17–19, NKJV). When he left home, he was strutting his stuff. He had his independence. He had money and a motorcycle full of gas. He was on his way to do his thing.

In the far country, he was living the good life called pleasure. When he lost all his money, he called it bad luck. But when he wound up with those stinking pigs, he looked into the mirror of reality and said, "I have sinned."

What is sin? The Bible says, "So whoever knows the right thing to do and fails to do it, for him it is sin" (James 4:17, ESV).

The Bible said the son "came to himself" (v. 17, NKJV). If he came to himself, that means he wasn't himself. If he was outside of himself, then he was insane. Sin is insanity. It is insane for you to believe that you can sin and get away with it. The Bible very clearly says that God will not allow sin to get into heaven, which is why it would be a good thing for you to pray the Lord's Prayer every single night before you go to bed because I'm sure you've done something that day for which you need to be cleaned up.

The father saw his boy coming down the road. He recognized the way he walked. He saw him in rags. The father ran down the dusty trail and met that boy while he was far off. Why? Because he didn't want the servants in the house to see what sin had done to his boy. Bring the robe! Bring the ring! Bring the shoes! I'm going to give them to him out here so that when he gets to the house he's going to look like a son and not a slave.

Now comes the older brother. Let's put him on the stand. Remember Jesus was telling the story here. Imagine Him looking at those self-righteous Pharisees, the ones who were judging Him for who He ate with. Jesus looked at them with fire in His eyes, knowing He was about to paint their portrait.

So much is said of the prodigal son, but the elder brother is by far the greatest sinner in this story.

Do you want to know why I think the prodigal left home? Not because of the attraction of the far country, but because of the cold, critical spirit of the older brother. I think people stay away from church in America because the Church many times becomes so judgmental, so critical, so Pharisaical, and many times downright loveless and self-righteous.

Hear the voice of Jesus: ". . . love one another as I have loved you" (John 15:12, NKJV). "By this all will know that you are My disciples, if you have love one for another" (John 13:35, NKJV). Two thousand years ago this is how they identified the church: by their love. That has not been said of the church of Jesus Christ for two thousand years, and it's time for that to become a reality. It's time to love each other to the point that the world will want to know what we have because of the way we care for each other.

These two sons represent the sin of passion (that's the prodigal) and the sin of disposition (the older brother).

We teach against the sin of passion relentlessly, yet seldom mention the sins of disposition.

We've been far harder on profanity than we have been on pride. But the Bible says the Lord resists the proud; pride goes before a fall; if you have a prideful spirit, God is opposed to you.

We've been far harder on adultery than the sin of accusation, gossip, and tale bearing. You should go through the Bible and read the verses about God dealing with talebearers. It's severe. Don't you dare lift your voice against a righteous person; you're talking about one of God's children.

We've been far harder on lust than we have the sin of legalism. Legalism is the keeping of manmade rules to obtain righteousness with God. To a degree, every denomination in America has its own form of legalism, things they do and don't do in order to be holy and pure. Let me tell you something: all of the rules that God wants you to follow are in His holy book.

Most of the people think of the elder brother as respectable compared to the prodigal brother — not so. It is true the older brother stayed home, but begrudgingly. He kept the rules, but he kept them grinding his teeth in total resentment. He joined the church. He sang in the choir. He sowed no wild oats. He wasted no money. But he was a sour, angry, bitter, mean-spirited, loveless, resentful, Bible-thumping sour puss.

If keeping manmade religious rules are necessary to obtain righteousness with God, why does God hate legalism? Because if you can be saved, Paul said, by the keeping of manmade rules, Jesus Christ died in vain (see Galatians 2:21). You are saved by what He did on the cross, not by the keeping of other people's rules.

When the prodigal came home, the elder brother reminded the father of all his brother's sins. He didn't say I'm glad my brother's home. He said I've kept the rules all these years; you haven't so much as killed an old goat for me. Yet you killed the fatted calf for this boy who wasted your money with prostitutes.

How did he know his brother had spent his money on prostitutes? Because that's what he would have done. Be careful what you say with your mouth, because it will expose you every time!

When the elder brother heard that the younger brother was home, the Bible said he was angry and would not go in. He heard the music, the mariachis playing. He smelled the barbacoa and the tacos and the carne asada. And he asked one of the hired hands, what does this mean? It means your younger brother has come home and your daddy is throwing a fiesta to top all fiestas.

If there is anything human in you at all, wouldn't you want to go home and celebrate the return of your brother? The Bible says it was not so of the older brother. He was angry and would not go in.

Listen closely to this next statement: *in rejecting his younger brother, the elder son lost fellowship with his father.*

The father was in the house, rejoicing that his boy had come home. And that sour puss legalist is out in the pasture, swelled up and angry, because the young man has confessed his sin and has come into the kingdom of God.

Two sons: the one who has been forgiven, who has come home, who has a new robe, a new ring, a new pair of shoes, and a bright future; and the rule-keeping sour puss out in the pasture with his fourteen-pound King James Bible keeping all the rules.

The story ends with the prodigal inside, the music so loud it is peeling the paint off the walls, and the elder brother outside, alone, joyless, and bitter, refusing to forgive the younger brother and separated from fellowship with the father. Where are you in the story?

Unity, in marriage and in families, is so very important and so very rare. This is the truth revealed in understanding the power of two.

– E I G H T –

THE POWER OF THE WORD

"That Book, sir, is the Rock on which our Republic rests." –ANDREW JACKSON[74]

"To read, truly read, a text, is not a cozy fireside chat between well-brought up people, in which one shares information, recalls memories, has a good time. Reading a text is a confrontation, a row, hand-to-hand fighting, which one can only leave marked and changed. It is Jacob wrestling with the angel (Gen 32:23–33), a bloody fight, which went through the night 'until daybreak'; an obstinate battle which refused to give up until it had obtained what it wanted: 'I will not let you go until you bless me'; a fight which left its mark, as it did on the patriarch's

hip; a fight, at the end of which, while the reader is not allowed to know the angel's name, Jacob still receives an unexpected revelation, in addition to the blessing, a new name which marks a change of identity." -ROLAND MEYNET[75]

Many years ago, on a flight home from Israel, I sat next to a Holocaust survivor named Sol Weinglass. He told me how he survived Hitler's hell, forced to endure Auschwitz where his entire family perished. I was riveted to his story, but one thing he said has stayed with me all these years. He said, "The Nazis controlled us with food." He said that they became experts in the signs of starvation to the point that they knew when a person would die. He didn't say anything about the physical symptoms — about how you could count every rib and their bellies would distend. He didn't even talk about how hungry they felt. He talked about the mental and emotional aspects. He said the signs of starvation were irritation, joylessness, depression, and finally, death.

I believe there is a spiritual parallel to what that remarkable holocaust survivor described. Have you ever met someone who looked like they'd had all the joy sucked out of them with a vacuum cleaner? Have you ever found yourself getting irritated over the least little thing; or no longer caring, even when you knew you should, even when you wanted to, but you just couldn't muster up the energy for it? If my friend Sol met you, he would say you were knocking on death's door.

The interesting thing about restoring victims of starvation is that you don't just start feeding them cheeseburgers and milkshakes to get them back to good health. You have to start slow, with IV fluids, then work them up to a small glass of milk and eventually solid food. Paul wrote to the Corinthian church, "I gave you milk, not solid food, for you were not yet ready for it. Indeed, you are still not ready" (1 Corinthians 3:2, NIV).

Paul saw the Corinthians as infants in Christ, not yet spiritually mature enough for solid food. Human infants start with breast milk, then pureed baby food in those little jars, and eventually work their way up to being teenagers who eat you out of house and home. But it's a process that takes time as your entire body learns how to work together to process food.

In the same way, you need to strengthen your spiritual body. If you put this book down and try to feast on the Bible, reading Genesis, Exodus, and Leviticus all in one sitting, your eyes will cross and you'll want to throw up because this food is so rich. No, you need to savor the morsels of it. Ask God to nourish your soul-sick body, one verse, ten minutes, at a time. My mouth is watering just thinking about you taking in the power of the Word and learning to crawl, walk, and finally run in the freedom, joy, hope, peace, patience, happiness, and energetic passion that are contained in the Holy Book!

Let's look at one such morsel. Jesus said, "It is written, 'Man shall not live by bread alone, but by every word that proceeds from the mouth of God'" (Matthew 4:4, NKJV). He was referring to the Old Testament, when the Israelites wandered in the wilderness desert for forty years as they learned to trust God. God fed them with a daily source of manna to teach them to daily rely on Him. But it wasn't the bread that sustained them, it was their Father in heaven.

It's possible that as you read this right now, you need to change your diet. You may be starving to death. Did you know that you can eat every day and still starve to death?[76] That's because it's not eating that gives life and good health, it's eating the right things. Nielson ratings showed that back in 2009–10, the average American adult watched almost nine hours of television a day.[77] Television is no longer a pastime. For many it constitutes more time than a full-time job!

Those numbers have gone down marginally in the past decade, but only to be replaced by Netflix, YouTube, social media, and other digital content. Imagine if you spent even a quarter of that time reading your Bible. You would be so much stronger, alert, and alive — you could change the world in your sleep! The Bible is your source of spiritual food and when you refuse to read it, you starve yourself of its life-giving power.

The opening words of the Gospel of John speak of Jesus: "In the beginning was the Word, and the Word was with God, and the Word was God" (John 1:1, KJV). The Word was from the beginning and the Word was Jesus. John 1:14 says, "And the Word became flesh and dwelt among us, and we have seen his glory, glory as of the only Son from the Father, full of grace and truth" (ESV). Jesus is the Word made flesh. He was the living, breathing Bible in human form. Therefore, when Jesus says that He is the hunger satisfier and thirst quencher, He is also speaking of the Scriptures:

And Jesus said to them, "I am the bread of life. He who comes to Me shall never hunger, and he who believes in Me shall never thirst." (John 6:35, NKJV)

In the same way, the Bible is the bread of life for the hungry. It is meat for men and milk for children. This Word is living water for those who thirst after righteousness.

Are you hungry for joy? Are you thirsty for peace? In the pages to come we'll sink our teeth into the power of the Word.

THREE THINGS YOU NEED TO KNOW

The Word of God is the most powerful weapon God has ever given to mortal flesh. This is the living, breathing, infallible, eternal, inerrant word of God. This is Holy Spirit inspired. This is the indestructible word of God. Tyrants have burned it. Dictators have demanded it be put aside. But it rises from the ashes to become the powerful source of truth to the nations of the world.

This is the gateway to the unsearchable riches of heaven. This is sharper than any two-edged sword, dividing marrow from the bone, truth from deception, light from darkness, sheep from goats, and victory from defeat. The Bible is the combat manual in spiritual warfare that guarantees victory over the world, the flesh, and the devil. Here paradise is restored, the gates of heaven are opened, and the gates of hell are closed.

Paul, the New Testament gospel's Commander in Chief, said to "Put on the whole armor of God, that you may be able to stand against the schemes of the devil" (Ephesians 6:11, ESV) and "fight the good fight of faith" (1 Timothy 6:12, NKJV).

King Solomon said, "The godly may trip seven times, but they will get up again" (Proverbs 24:16, NLT). In other words, if you get knocked down six times, get up seven times. That was not some fortune cookie saying. That was King Solomon, the wisest man who ever lived, who told you to fight to the finish, fight to win, and don't stop fighting until you do. You're never defeated until you refuse to get up. You have the authority of God's name and the power of the Word to get back up again. Stay in the fight! Fight to win; victory is yours in Jesus Christ.

When Jesus went into the desert and was tempted by the devil, what did He use to fight back? He used the weapon of the Word. He said, "It is written . . ." Three times Jesus fought back with those words: "It is written," and He pushed the devil out (see Matthew 4:4, 7, 10).

The devil is after you, no doubt about it. But God has given you an arsenal to drive the devil out. Use the power of the Word to drive the devil out of your mind, your marriage, out of your business, out of your church, out of the government. Get him out! You are an overcomer because "He who is in you is greater than he who is in the world" (1 John 4:4, NKJV). Proclaim the Word and victory is yours. Let God arise and let His enemies be scattered.

There are three things you need to know about the Holy Bible: (1) we **read** it to be wise; (2) we **believe** it to be saved; (3) we **practice** it to be holy. We understand wisdom and salvation, but why should you be concerned about holiness? Because the Bible says, "Pursue peace with all people, and holiness, without which no one will see the Lord" (Hebrews 12:14, NKJV). Do you want to see God one day, sitting on that heavenly throne surrounded by angels and pearly gates and streets made out of gold? Then you better be concerned with living a holy life.

The story goes that a father and son from an affluent neighborhood went car shopping. The son was getting ready to graduate from high school and his dad had promised to buy him a car for graduation. Every weekend, father and son went to different dealerships until finally, a week before graduation, the son found his dream car. After walking across the stage and receiving his diploma, the son couldn't wait to get home and take his new car for a spin! Instead of car keys, however, his father handed him a gift-wrapped Bible. The son was so mad that his dad had gone back on his promise to buy him a car that he stormed out and never spoke to his dad again. Years later, when he came home for his father's funeral, he discovered that Bible amongst his father's belongings. Opening the Bible for the first time, the son discovered a check, dated the day of his high school graduation, for the full amount of the car that they had picked out together.[78]

If only the son had known the power of the Word! The Word of God is the greatest book ever written. The Bible is greater than all other books like the ocean is greater than the water that drips from the faucet in your kitchen. It is greater than other books like the blazing sun is greater than the feeble glow of a child's birthday cake candle. It is greater than all other books like the Rocky Mountains are greater than a grain of sand in your backyard. There is more horsepower in one passage of the Bible than in all the Lamborghinis in the world. Abraham Lincoln, our sixteenth president who many consider our greatest president, said, "In regard for this Great Book, I have this to say, it is the best gift God has given to man. All the good Savior gave to the world was communicated through this Book."[79] Lincoln held the union together when it was shattering because he knew the power of the Word.

TRUE NORTH

A true story was shared with me about a Christian speaker who was invited to a secular university to defend the reality of God. As he walked to the podium, he instantly recognized the hostility of the audience. He knew he had to come at them with a different approach, so he said, "I want everyone to stand up and point north." Hundreds of students stood up and pointed all different directions like the scarecrow in the Wizard of Oz. Some pointed up. Others to their right or left or behind them. When they had all returned to their seats he reached into his pocket and pulled out a compass. He told them that God had created the world with a magnetic field so that the compass would always point north.

The Bible is the moral compass for the nations. It will always point us to true north. It will always take us back to greatness. Solomon wrote, "Righteousness exalts a nation, but sin is a reproach to any people" (Proverbs 14:34, NKJV). All nations that forget God will be turned into hell, but those who follow true north will be exalted.

The Bible is the moral compass of the soul. The Word of God "is a lamp to my feet and a light to my path" (Psalm 119:105, NKJV). It shows me both the next step and the end goal of where I'm going.

The Bible contains the mind of God. You want to know what God thinks? Read the Holy Scriptures.

The Bible is the Magna Carta of happiness for believers. Its doctrines are holy. Its precepts are binding. Its histories are true. And its decisions are immutable. "Immutable" means that according to God's law it cannot be changed. It is the whole truth and nothing but the truth.

Isaiah 2:3 declares, "The law will go out from Zion, the word of the LORD from Jerusalem" (NIV). There is going to come a day when the Judge of all judges will sit on His eternal throne and open the Book to send forth His Word. He's not sending out fake news; it will be chapter and verse what comes out of this sacred text.

Isaiah 40:8 proclaims, "The grass withers, the flower fades, but the word of our God will stand forever" (Isaiah 40:8, ESV). Note that last word: *forever*. Long after America no longer exists and Europe has been crushed by the Antichrist, one thing will remain: the Word of God.

This is not a passing trend. It isn't a hairstyle from the nineties or bellbottoms of the seventies, coming in and out of style. No. This is honey in the rock that satisfies the soul, and it will stand forever.

Other books you read may impress you, but the Bible will change you. It will make you a new creature in Christ Jesus. You can read Shakespeare, Shelley, Keats, Byron, Longfellow — in fact, you should! But they will not change you. From time to time, they will flat out bore you. But when you read creation's story in Genesis, when you turn the page to Exodus and read the miracles of an Almighty God leading two million Jewish people out of Egyptian bondage, dividing the Red Sea, guiding them with a cloud by day and warming them with a fire by night, providing manna six days a week, when you read Matthew, Mark, Luke, and John — it will change you.

The Bible is a chain breaker, habit breaker, past breaker. It makes sinners forsake their ways. It takes the pain out of dying. It takes the gloom from the grave and gives a hope that is steadfast and sure. When Jesus said, "Because I live, you also will live" (John 14:19, ESV), He meant that one day every righteous grave on the face of the earth is going to explode and the dead will be awakened and rise to meet the King of Glory in the air. What a wonderful day that will be!

THE BIBLE'S ONE WEAKNESS

Goliath was a giant with brute strength. Yet he was brought down by young David's sling and a single pebble. Samson had the strength to tear apart a lion with his bare hands. Yet his love for Delilah and a simple haircut brought about his demise. Superman's kryptonite was his Achilles' heel. Every warrior has his weakness.

The Bible is filled with power: the power to overcome death, hell and the grave, the power to throw open the gates of heaven, the power to give life and joy and peace and hope in hopeless circumstances. Yet it has one weakness. That weakness is this: most of the people who call themselves Christians don't read the Bible.

You've heard the saying, "If a tree falls in the woods and no one is there to hear it, does it make a sound?" The same could be said of the Bible, "If the Word of God is filled with power but no one takes the time to open it, does it imbue power?" Plenty of Christians carry their Bibles to church on Sunday. They might even have a stack of translations on their office shelf or out on the coffee table for the neighbors to see. But if they never take the time to read it, it doesn't do them any good.

It was previously stated that the average adult watches almost nine hours of television a day. Yet how many hours does the average adult read the Bible? Studies show that one-third of Americans report reading the Bible once a week and one-half report reading their Bible at least once a month.[80] Television reports come out in the number of hours *a day*, but Bible reading is reported by the number of times read in *a month*.

Something is wrong with this picture! It is no wonder so many people are living without the power of God activated in their lives. The same study shows that sixty percent of people wish they read their Bibles more.[81] Well, you can't wish your way to power any more than you can wish your way into heaven. Either you open the book and receive power, or you don't!

People want to know why their lives are falling apart. Well, the proof is in the pudding. People who have a Bible that's falling apart, have a life that's not falling apart. Let me say that again: *People who have a Bible that's falling apart, have a life that's not falling apart.* To anyone who thinks they can't understand the Bible, let me say this: you have to read it to understand it. It's as simple as that.

The Bible is the Bread of Life. It is Living Water for the thirsty. If you don't consume the Word, you'll become what I call an anemic Christian. You won't have any energy or zest for life. You won't have the strength to do battle. You won't have joy or hope or peace. You'll die of spiritual starvation. And that's a fact.

HIDDEN IN THE HEART

Are you currently in a crisis? If you're not now, you either just got out of one, or I can guarantee one is coming. Grab your umbrella because that's a forecast you can count on. Among Jesus's famous last words to His disciples were these: "In the world ye shall have tribulation" (John 16:33, KJV). Ye shall. You will. Count on it! But hot on the heels of "trouble is coming," Jesus said, "but be of good cheer." Be of good cheer! Celebrate! Sing in the rain! Trials and sorrows are your future, but don't worry! Why? Because "I have overcome the world" (see John 16:33). The victory is ours!

The power of the Word is greater than the storms of life. When the storm hit on the Sea of Galilee and the twelve disciples were tossed about the ship, the sails were ripped to shreds and the boat filled with water. These seasoned fishermen feared for their lives, while Jesus took a nap, lulled to sleep by the crashing waves.

"Then He arose and rebuked the wind, and said to the sea, 'Peace, be still!' And the wind ceased and there was a great calm" (Mark 4:39, NKJV). A better translation is, "Be muzzled! Peace, be still!" That is power. Jesus had the power to calm the storm and he says that everything he did we can do, and even greater things than these.

David wrote, "Thy word have I hid in mine heart, that I might not sin against thee" (Psalm 119:11, KJV).

With the Word of God hidden in your heart, you have the power to speak to your storms, to muzzle them in the name of Jesus and proclaim, "Peace, be still!"

Jesus said, "Assuredly, I say to you, whatever you bind on earth will be bound in heaven, and whatever you loose on earth will be loosed in heaven" (Matthew 18:18, NKJV). When you pray and bind something in Jesus's name, it causes an instant response from heaven. God can stop what's happening on earth because you prayed. When you pray and loose something on earth, it is liberated in heaven according to the Word of God. That makes you more powerful than the Supreme Court of the United States. You have the authority to lay hands on the sick and make them recover. You have the authority to cast out demons with a word. You have the authority to declare war on the powers and principalities in the heavenlies. You have the power to determine your destiny in the power of the God we serve simply by hiding His Word in your heart.

PROVISION IN THE PROMISE

Where should you go to find heavenly provision for your needs? God's provisions are in His promises. There are three thousand promises in the Bible. That is three thousand ways that God has of blessing you. Paul wrote, "For no matter how many promises God has made, they are

'Yes' in Christ. And so through him the 'Amen' is spoken by us to the glory of God" (2 Corinthians 1:20, NIV). All the promises of God are yes and amen but none of them apply to you if you don't read the book. If you don't know it, you can't confess it, and until you can confess it, it's not yours.

Are you looking for a Friend? The Bible says Jesus "is a friend who sticks closer than a brother" (Proverbs 18:24, KJV).

Are you in a day of trouble when everyone, even your own family, has turned their back on you? The Bible says, "For my father and my mother have forsaken me, but the LORD will take me in" (Psalm 27:10, ESV).

Are you looking for hope? David said, "Why are you in despair, O my soul? And why have you become disturbed within me? Hope in God, for I shall again praise Him For the help of His presence" (Psalm 42:5, NASB). And he said, "But you, O LORD, are a shield about me, my glory, and the lifter of my head" (Psalm 3:3, ESV). What does that mean? That means that God leans off His throne and puts His hand under your chin and lifts your head to encourage you, to remind you to fix your eyes on Him because He is your "ever-present help in times of trouble" (Psalm 46:1, BSB).

Are you looking for joy? The Bible says, "In Your presence is fullness of joy" (Psalm 16:11, NKJV), and "weeping may endure for a night, but joy cometh in the morning" (Psalm 30:5, KJV).

Are you in need of victory? The Bible says, "But thanks be to God, who gives us the victory through our Lord Jesus Christ" (1 Corinthians 15:57, NKJV).

Are you looking for health and healing? Isaiah 53:5 says, "But He was wounded for our transgressions, He was bruised for our iniquities; the chastisement for our peace was upon Him, and by His stripes we are healed" (NKJV). Jesus was the Great Physician. He is still the Great Physician and will always be the Great Physician. When He was on this earth, He healed one-on-one. He healed en masse. He healed with His saliva because Judaism taught that there was healing power in the spittle of the firstborn Son. Jesus was demonstrating He was the first-born Son of the Father in heaven.

I'm not going to go through all three thousand promises because you need to read them and receive them for yourself. I won't do all the work for you, but I will tell you this. We have made church way too complicated. All we really need to do is get our lives in harmony with the anointing of the Holy Spirit by laying hold of the promises in the Word and the world will be attracted to the awesome power that God brings to His church.

On the day of their ordination, Jesus told His disciples to go out and preach, to heal the sick and raise the dead and cast out demons, and you know what? They did.

It didn't take all day for them to get the message. They went and turned the world upside down, and we are told to do the same. When we release the power of the Word of God, our lives will be rich and happy and filled with His purposes.

#BLESSED

King David said, "Bless the LORD, O my soul, and forget not all his benefits" (Psalm 103:2, KJV). What are the benefits of knowing God and His Word? David tells us in the very next verse. First, David says, God "forgives all your iniquities" (v. 3, NKJV).

What is the difference between a sin and an iniquity? You can actually commit a sin and not be conscious of it, but an iniquity is something you do on purpose. You sin, and you know it's a sin, and yet you do it anyway.

Have you ever said, "I know I shouldn't tell you this, but . . .", or "I know I shouldn't eat this, but . . .", or "I know I shouldn't do this, but . . ."? Anytime you say, "I know I shouldn't, but . . .", it's an iniquity. You knew it was wrong even while you did it.

David knew what he was talking about. He planned the murder of his friend Uriah because he wanted Uriah's wife, Bathsheba. David knew it was wrong, but he did it anyway. He did it, and God forgave his iniquity. Now don't take that as a license to sin on purpose, because forgiveness does not mean there aren't consequences.

David's heart was sick over what he'd done, and then his newborn baby died, and he wasn't even allowed to build the temple to worship God. God forgave him but there was still a price to pay. There was a great deal of blessing ahead for David, including the birth of his son Solomon, but his iniquity was not without repercussions.

This is the God "Who redeems your life from destruction, who crowns you with lovingkindness and tender mercies" (Psalm 103:4, NKJV). His forgiveness is such lovingkindness; his correction is a tender mercy. This is the God "Who satisfies your mouth with good things, So that your youth is renewed like the eagle's" (v. 5, NKJV). Is this wetting your palette yet? You need to get into the Word. It is so rich.

This Book is the birthplace of blessing. You were born to be blessed. Every person was born to be blessed. Follow the blessing of God in the Bible: God blessed Adam and Eve in the Garden. They broke covenant with God and God cast them out of the Garden. Noah's generation failed God, and God wiped that generation off the face of the earth with a flood, all except for Noah and his family who were blessed.

Then God found a man by the name of Abraham whom He could trust. God made a covenant with Abraham and his children and his children's children. Abraham's son

Isaac was blessed. Isaac's son Jacob was blessed. Jacob gathered his twelve sons around his death bed and blessed each one. Those twelves sons and the blessings they were given controlled the history of the nation of Israel for the next thousand years.

To open the Book of Psalms, David wrote, "BLESSED is the man that walketh not in the counsel of the ungodly, nor standeth in the way of sinners, nor sitteth in the seat of the scornful. But his delight is in the law of the LORD; and in his law doth he meditate day and night" (Psalm 1:1–2, KJV, emphasis added).

How did Jesus begin His ministry? With the beatitudes: "BLESSED are the poor in spirit; BLESSED are they that mourn; BLESSED are the meek; BLESSED are they which do hunger and thirst after righteousness; BLESSED are the merciful; BLESSED are the pure in heart; BLESSED are the peacemakers; BLESSED are they which are persecuted for righteousness' sake; BLESSED are ye . . ." (see Matthew 5:3–11, KJV, emphasis added).

Paul begins his letter to the Ephesians: "BLESSED be the God and Father of our Lord Jesus Christ, who hath BLESSED us with all spiritual BLESSINGS in heavenly places in Christ" (Ephesians 1:3, KJV, emphasis added).

John, from the island of Patmos, opens the book of Revelation: "BLESSED is the one who reads aloud the words of this prophecy, and BLESSED are those who hear, and who keep what is written in it, for the time is near" (Revelation 1:3, ESV, emphasis added). BLESSED. BLESSED. BLESSED.

The blessings of God move throughout Scripture, from the gates of Genesis to the closing of Revelation. God wants to bless you, and He does so through His Word. Not through social media hashtags or t-shirt slogans or "bless your heart" platitudes which, if you didn't know already, aren't actually a compliment. Blessings come through the Word, so if you don't read His book, you don't know what He can give you. But when you read the Word, He'll bless you out of your socks!

YOU ARE WHAT YOU EAT

We started this chapter talking about food. If that was our appetizer, this is our dessert! "Oh, taste and see that the LORD is good; BLESSED is the man who trusts in Him!" (Psalm 34:8, NKJV, emphasis added).

The Word of God is the chocolate cake a la mode with a cherry on top that God wants to use to infuse your life with power. It's the pecan pie, banana pudding, peach cobbler, Texas cheesecake of your dreams.

Paul calls it the breath of God. Jesus calls it daily bread. Like daily bread it must be consumed on a regular basis to be of any good to you. What is it good for? Paul says the Scriptures are "useful for teaching, rebuking, correcting and training in righteousness, so that the servant of God may be thoroughly equipped for every good work" (2 Timothy 3:16–17, NIV). The Bible is your power source for every good thing you are called to do for the kingdom. It strengthens you, trains you, gets you back on track when your train derails, and equips you to live a life in service to God.

Have you ever heard the saying, *You are what you eat*? Adam and Eve ate forbidden fruit, and they were cast out of the Garden. John the Baptist ate locusts and wild honey and was known as Jesus's eccentric cousin from Judea. Revelation 22:2 says, "In the middle of its street, and on either side of the river, was the tree of life, which bore twelve fruits, each tree yielding its fruit every month. The leaves of the tree were for the healing of the nations" (NKJV). In the heavenly realm there are twelve fruits, one for every month, and when you eat them you eat your way to health and healing.

Romans 15:4 says, "For whatever things were written before were written for our learning, that we through the patience and comfort of the Scriptures might have hope" (NKJV). While joylessness, weakness, and despair are signs of spiritual starvation, hope is a sign of spiritual strength.

Your power comes from reading the Word of God, but if you aren't wielding that two-edged sword, you aren't equipped for battle. Your joy comes from studying the Word of God, but if you aren't immersing yourself in it, you'll never have the joy unspeakable and full of glory that Scripture promises.

Your hope comes from believing the Word of God, but if you aren't professing it, you'll never truly know the One who can be trusted to keep His promises. Jesus said, "Heaven and earth shall pass away, but my words shall not pass away" (Matthew 24:35, KJV). The Word "comes from the mouth of God" (Matthew 4:4, ESV) and is the very "inspiration of God" (2 Timothy 3:16, KJV). Life is in the Word, and it's yours if you dare to read it.

THE POWER OF THE HOLY SPIRIT

God Almighty, Creator of heaven and earth, also flung the stars against the velvet of the night on creation's morning. Who calls the stars by name? Who holds the seven seas in the palm of His hand? Whose voice can split the cedars of Lebanon? This one true God is the God of absolute power and He wants to share that power with you.

Jesus told his disciples,

> *"Behold, I send the Promise of my Father upon you, but tarry in Jerusalem until you be endued with power from on high."* (Luke 24:49)

Our world is intoxicated with its endless quest and craving for power. More is better. Brilliant scientists have created nuclear weapons so powerful that millions of people can be charred to an ash in fractions of a second. On planet earth, multiple nations now have the power to cremate civilization several times over. It is a fact of history that never has a military weapon been invented that has not been used to destroy both lives and homes.

The endless lust for power is demonstrated every fall in America when millions of intelligent people pack huge football stadiums to watch powerful gladiators of the twenty-first century demolish each other. The wounded are carried from the field of battle as celebrated heroes to the applause of thousands. Power is indeed intoxicating!

Two highly trained boxers whose bodies are chiseled portraits of power climb into a roped arena to physically destroy each other. One delivers a knockout punch which produces such neurological trauma to the other's brain that the body collapses on the canvas. The winner will be awarded a championship belt and tens of millions of dollars for this "civilized" gladiator of the ring.

Almost everything is celebrated or eliminated because of the power factor. Men buy cars because of power. Military might that defends our life, liberty, and pursuit of happiness is measured by the power factor. Men, who couldn't hit the broadside of a barn if they were locked inside it, fill their gun cases with powerful guns and expensive scopes.

The greatest power in the universe is overlooked by our television and cell phone addicted society. This awesome power has the ability to guide you personally into all truth. It has the power to raise you from the dead. It has the power to bring all things to your remembrance, and when you pass age seventy that's a major miracle!

It has the power to heal sick bodies and break the chains of addictive habits that enslave human beings. This power brings peace to the tormented mind and unshakable hope to the brokenhearted.

This awesome and unlimited *power* is the *person* of the Holy Spirit of God who is waiting for you to invite Him into your life.

THE PROMISE

The promise of the Holy Spirit was made by Jesus Christ to His disciples on the Mount of Olives in Jerusalem just before He was taken up and a cloud received Him out of their sight. The promise reads:

> *"But you shall receive power when the Holy Spirit has come upon you; and you shall be witnesses to Me in Jerusalem, and in all Judea and Samaria, and to the end of the earth."* (Acts 1:8, NKJV)

As I noted in the previous chapter, the provisions of God are in the promises of God. We also observed that there are about three thousand promises in the Word of God destined to enrich and empower your life. There is no power on the earth greater than the Holy Spirit because the Holy Spirit is God. The symbol of the Holy Spirit is the dove which descended on the shoulder of Jesus Christ when He was baptized in the Jordan River by John the Baptist.

When you invite the Holy Spirit into your life you will immediately have access to unlimited power, equipping you to know what others cannot know, to say what others cannot say, and to do what others cannot do. These three things are accomplished through the gifts of the Holy Spirit which are available to every believer.

Paul refers to this in 1 Corinthians 12:7–11,

But the manifestation of the Spirit is given to each one for the profit of all: for to one is given the word of wisdom through the Spirit, to another the word of knowledge through the same Spirit, to another faith by the same Spirit, to another gifts of healings by the same Spirit, to another the working of miracles, to another prophecy, to another discerning of spirits, to another different kinds of tongues, to another the interpretation of tongues. But one and the same

Spirit works all these things, distributing to each one individually as He [the Holy Spirit] wills. (NKJV)

Read this verse carefully and absorb every word and you will have taken a baby step toward beginning to grasp the magnitude of the power of the Holy Spirit to transform your life forever.

THE HOVERING POWER IN CREATION

The Holy Spirit appears in Genesis 1:1 with the words, "In the beginning God . . ." "In the beginning" refers to the dateless past, before time began. Time did not begin until God created the sun and the moon to calculate a twenty-four-hour solar day.

The Holy Spirit appears with the words, "In the beginning God" because the original word for "God" in the text is *Elohim*, which is the plural form of "El," implying a plurality of persons in Creation. Simply stated, this refers to the Trinity: The Father, the Son, and the Holy Spirit.

The Trinity appears again in Genesis 1:26, with the words, "Let US make man in OUR image" (KJV, emphasis added). The Holy Spirit must never be referred to as "It." The Holy Spirit is God, coequal with the Father and the Son.

The "hovering" of the Holy Spirit is seen in Genesis 1:2, with the words, "And the Spirit of God was hovering over the face of the waters" (NKJV). The gap between verse 1 — *"in the beginning God created the heavens and the earth"* — and verse 2 — *"the Spirit of God was hovering over the face of the waters"* — could have been millions of years.

If your college professor tells you that scientists have carbon dated a rock to 50,000 years ago, that is completely possible. There is no time clock between Genesis 1:1 and Genesis 1:2. The earth was in a state of void for an indeterminate amount of time. Then verse 2 comes along and the Holy Spirit re-enters the story and He hovers over the earth. It is while He is hovering over the earth that supernatural power is released.

The Holy Spirit is a hovering force that brings supernatural power to you and to everything you touch. The hovering of the Holy Spirit turned darkness into light. The hovering of the Holy Spirit brought order out of chaos. The hovering of the Holy Spirit divided the land from the water, and the oceans were retained by the continents that rose up. The hovering represents the creative splendor of the Lord Himself as He flung the stars against the velvet of the night to be glittering evangelists to the world.

THE HOLY SPIRIT IN THE VIRGIN BIRTH

When the Holy Spirit hovered over the Virgin Mary, a sacred seed from heaven was planted in her womb, producing Jesus Christ who crushed the head of the serpent (see Matthew 1:18, 20).

The power of the Holy Spirit in the birth of Jesus cannot be underestimated. It is this Jesus, the Son of David and the Son of Abraham, who went to Calvary and bled and died for your redemption and mine.

It is this Jesus that the Bible presents as the Lion of the Tribe of Judah, the Rose of Sharon, the Fairest of Ten Thousand, the Great Shepherd of the Church, and the Great I Am. He is the God of all hope, and He is soon to return to this earth to establish a glorious kingdom that shall never end.

John the Baptist, who came specifically to introduce Jesus, presented Jesus as the baptizer in the Holy Spirit: "I [John the Baptist] baptize you with water for repentance. But after me comes one who is more powerful than I, whose sandals I am not worthy to carry. He [Jesus] will baptize you with the Holy Spirit and fire" (Matthew 3:11, NIV). John says that Jesus baptizes with two things: with the Holy Spirit and with fire. Both were experienced on the day of Pentecost in the Upper Room.

Creation began with the hovering of the Holy Spirit over the waters. The birth of Jesus began with the hovering of the Holy Spirit over the Virgin Mary. The New Testament Church began with the hovering of the Holy Spirit over the disciples.

When do miracles begin in your life? When God's children come together in the House of the Lord and begin to praise him. The Bible says, "But thou art holy, O thou that inhabitest the praises of Israel" (Psalm 22:3, KJV). *To inhabit* is to "live in," so the Lord lives in the praises of His people. As we praise Him in our churches, the Holy Spirit hovers over our congregations, and the Holy Spirit power to do miracles is set in motion.

When you get in the sweet presence of the hovering of the Holy Spirit, chains of habits that enslave are broken, sick bodies are healed, disease is conquered, and broken hearts are flooded with joy unspeakable and full of glory. That's when the troubled heart finds peace that surpasses understanding. That's when the weak are made strong. That's when those who mourn are comforted. That's when peace drives out fear. That's when unshakable hope drives out despair and God's love drives out hatred. You are not living until you get in the hovering presence of the Holy Spirit and let Him reenergize and refresh you in your heart, soul, mind, and body.

THE POWER TO WITNESS

The Holy Spirit empowers you to be a witness for Jesus Christ. Jesus said to His disciples:

> *"But when the Comforter is come, whom I will send unto you from the Father, even the Spirit of truth, which proceedeth from the Father, he shall testify of me: And ye also shall bear witness, because ye have been with me from the beginning."* (John 15:26–27, KJV)

The power of the Holy Spirit to witness is not to testify about your denomination, your church, your dreams, or your visions. No, it is given to bear witness about the goodness, the mercy, and the grace of God received at the moment of your salvation.

The Holy Spirit experience in Acts 2 was God's FedEx to the Church that Jesus had arrived in heaven. While Jesus was on the earth, He spoke to His disciples and said:

> *"These things I have spoken to you while being present with you. But the Helper, the Holy Spirit, whom the Father will send in My name, He will teach you all things, and bring to your remembrance all things that I said to you."* (John 14:25–26, NKJV)

When the disciples were gathered in the Upper Room, God the Father sent the Holy Spirit and cloven tongues of fire sat upon the heads of 120 believers who were imbued with the supernatural power to witness for Christ.

Why were there 120 people in the Upper Room? Because there are twelve tribes of Israel and Jewish law required that ten people be present to have an official prayer meeting. Ten times twelve is 120, symbolizing a national prayer meeting for the nation of Israel to be filled with the Holy Spirit.

There was no television, radio, or Gutenberg Press to reach all of these nations. But because they were all gathered in one place, in the Upper Room, there was a supernatural anointing on these people. These 120 people left the Upper Room and went into the streets and spoke in the native tongue of the visitors to the city of Jerusalem who were evangelized to recognize Jesus Christ as the Son of God.

Think about that kind of power. This was the first official evangelism explosion in the New Testament. This was an evangelism explosion par excellence; beyond anything anyone could possibly imagine. Because of that evangelism explosion, 3,000 people got saved in one day.

Some people believe that the Day of Pentecost in Acts 2 was the first Day of Pentecost. Not true! The Jewish people had been celebrating the Day of Pentecost from Mount Sinai, 1,500 years before Acts 2 was ever written.

God told Moses to bring the children of Israel from Egypt's bondage to the Promised Land to come to this mountain. Here Moses spoke with God face-to-face as tongues of fire covered the mountain and seventy languages were spoken.

Why was it called Pentecost? Pentecost is from the Greek word *pentekostos*, which means "fifty." It was a fifty-day journey from the Red Sea where God miraculously delivered them from the bondage of Pharaoh and Egypt to Mount Sinai. It was here the nation of Israel was born.

Fifteen hundred years later, in the Upper Room in Jerusalem, cloven tongues of fire sat upon the head of every believer in a national prayer meeting and the New Testament Church was born. The Day of Pentecost is the birthday of the New Testament Church.

POWER FOR THE BELIEVER

The Holy Spirit was God's promise to the Church to have power to carry the Gospel with signs and wonders to the ends of the earth:

> *But ye shall receive power, after that the Holy Ghost is come upon you: and ye shall be witnesses unto me both in Jerusalem, and in all Judaea, and in Samaria, and unto the uttermost part of the earth. (Acts 1:8, KJV)*

One of the purposes of the Holy Spirit was to produce a church with POWER! The Lord's Prayer establishes that point: "For thine is the kingdom, and the power, and the glory, for ever. . . ." (Matthew 6:13, KJV).

Jesus said to His disciples, and He is saying to you the reader, "All power is given unto me in heaven and in earth" (Matthew 28:18, KJV), *and I give you that power.*

Again, God's provisions are in God's promises. God has promised every Holy Spirit filled person power over sickness and disease, power over demon spirits and witchcraft, power over principalities in the heavenlies for spiritual warfare.

We have power to get wealth, power to speak with authority, power to have supernatural knowledge, and power to make Holy Spirit inspired proclamations of prophecy. There is the power of praise that releases the anointing of the Holy Spirit and the power that shakes the gates of hell.

The Bible records these words concerning the New Testament believers: "And when they had prayed, the place where they were assembled together was shaken [power manifested]; and they were all filled with the Holy Spirit, and they spoke the word of God with boldness" (Acts 4:31, KJV).

Lord God of Israel, send the power of the Holy Spirit to the churches of America and to believers everywhere that a revival of righteousness can be born to a nation that has lost its moral compass!

It is my belief that the people in America are hungry to see the manifestations of the power of God. Let me share with you this personal illustration.

While preaching a crusade in Pennsylvania years ago at a large arena, a newspaper reporter came to get an interview from me concerning the thousands of people who were attending the event.

I asked the reporter, "Are you a believer?" He immediately responded, "No, actually I'm an atheist."

I pressed the question, "Why would your newspaper send an atheist to cover a religious event?" He responded that he was one of the leading reporters for his newspaper and was simply assigned to cover the event.

I did not drop the issue. I asked him a personal and direct question: "What would it take for you to believe there was a God?"

Without hesitation, he let me know that he and his wife had been trying to have a baby for many years and were unable to conceive. I told him to bring his wife to the service the next night and I would pray for God to give them a baby.

He looked at me in disbelief and our eyes locked. Finally, he said, "I'll do just that."

The next night the reporter and his wife appeared backstage before the services began. I talked to both of them, stating that God has the power to give life. They looked back at me with blank stares. I prayed the prayer and they left the arena.

About two years later, I was preaching another event in the area. I was in the greenroom with my security before the service was to begin. There was a knock at the door and the security officer stated that there was a member of the press who wished to speak with me.

I told him I was not interested in giving an interview just before I went out to preach. The security guard relayed that this was not an interview request, but that I had prayed for this reporter and his wife to have a baby.

I agreed to see him.

The door opened and the first thing through the door was a baby buggy with two beautiful twin girls inside. Pushing the stroller was the newspaper reporter and his wife. The blank stares from two years prior were now replaced with ear-to-ear smiles.

They had discovered the power of God to do what they thought was impossible, and God delivered. What is it in your life that you would like for God to do for you and your family? The Bible says, "ye have not, because ye ask not" (James 4:2, KJV). It also says, "All things are possible for one who believes" (Mark 9:23, ESV). Why don't you, right now, ask God to give you the thing in your life that you feel is impossible. Believe in the God who believes in you!

THE HOLY SPIRIT BRINGS UNITY

The last prayer Jesus prayed before He was taken into heaven was that the Church would be unified. Unity is not when we all think alike. Unity is when we can fellowship with people of like precious faith and allow them the freedom to have differences of opinion with us.

St. Paul writes,

> *For by one Spirit we were all baptized into one body — whether Jews or Greeks, whether slaves or free — and have all been made to drink into one Spirit.* (1 Corinthians 12:13, NKJV)

We must realize that Paul's main emphasis was not on doctrine, but on the unity of the body of Christ. God's primary purpose for bestowing the baptism of the Holy Spirit is the unity of the Church.

We have responded in our generation with dozens of denominations which wouldn't consider fellowship with other denominations because of one specific doctrine of difference that has nothing to do with redemption, and only results in separation.

Some denominations present the outpouring of the Holy Spirit as an emotional and undisciplined process of worship in the Church. This is not in the Bible.

Check it out for yourself! There is no specific reference to emotion in the various places in Scripture where the baptism of the Holy Spirit is written of or described. The Holy Spirit brings unity.

America is on the verge of collapse because of the lack of unity. There is lack of unity in the family and in our marriages. There is lack of unity in our churches. There is lack of unity in our nation where our Congress is in constant confusion concerning the true needs of the American people.

In our "land of the free" and "home of the brave," we have a shadow government trying to destroy the duly elected government. We have a leftist media pouring out "fake news" designed to destroy the confidence of the American people in our country.

Anarchists rule the streets in some of America's major cities. Policemen are being shot; lawlessness abounds. As a nation we are experiencing mass murder in churches and synagogues. Shopping malls and public schools have become killing fields for domestic terrorists.

In colleges and universities, speakers who profess Judeo-Christian values are shouted down. Speakers who defend constitutional government are harassed by socialists in the student body and faculty.

If you defend Israel, or the Jewish people, you are called a racist and a hatemonger.

Speakers that present the principles of socialism are applauded. *The Daily Caller* reports that one in three millennials see communism as favorable, and seventy percent will cast their vote for a socialist. [82]

When we fail to educate our younger generation on the principles of righteousness, and the historic truth that 100 million people were murdered by communists in the past century, we should not be surprised at their willingness to embrace the endless "promises" of socialism. Socialism has never worked in history. It begins with glorious promises and ends with a dictator producing a bloodbath for the nation.

Unity is a priceless treasure and America does not have that treasure right now. Many of you reading this book do not have unity in your personal life, in your marriage, or your home. Unity is a treasure presented by the presence of the Holy Spirit.

The solution for America is to remember that, "The wicked shall be turned into hell, and all the nations that forget God" (Psalm 9:17, KJV). Hell on earth is exactly what we have going on in the streets of America today. But we know the solution. The solution is the outpouring of the Holy Spirit in our pulpits, our churches, our families, our classrooms, and our streets, until there is a floodtide of unity replacing racism, socialism, paganism, humanism and anti-Semitism.

It's time for "we the people" to unite to make America what our founding fathers intended, based on the moral compass of the Word of God. We are still "one nation under God" and that God is the God of Abraham, Isaac, and Jacob; there is no other.

Let the wind and fire of the Holy Spirit sweep through your life, through your family, through your church, until this nation has a righteous revolution where truth is restored, and deception is destroyed.

THE HOLY SPIRIT IS OUR HELPER

Jesus Christ said to His disciples, "And I will ask the Father, and he will give you another Helper, to be with you forever" (John 14:16, ESV).

The Holy Spirit is called in this text a "Helper," but the Greek text is much stronger. The Greek word for "helper" is *parakletos*, which means, "a counselor, an advocate, a comforter, or an attorney."

The Bible presents the Holy Spirit as an all-knowing Counselor who shows you, personally, what to do when you don't know what to do. Have you ever been there? Are you there right now? If not, you will be!

The Bible clearly teaches that the Holy Spirit will tell you what to say when you don't know what to say. The Holy Spirit will give you revelation knowledge about what's going to happen in the future. In my sixty-plus years of ministry I have had this experience many times.

I vividly recall one particularly occasion. It was a Monday morning in my office at the first church we had built in San Antonio. I had finished my prayer time and sat down in my chair behind my desk. And out of the blue I received this very definite message from the Holy Spirit: "You will be attacked, but you will not be harmed."

It was so clear! So totally unexpected! As I sat behind the desk, I first believed it would be a media attack. It turned out to be a physical attack.

Three nights later, while I was teaching the Wednesday night service, a demonized madman with a gun came up the aisle and stopped about ten feet from the pulpit. He shouted, "I have come to kill you in front of this congregation to prove that Satan has more power than Jesus Christ!"

I responded as I held up my Bible, "This book declares that 'no weapon that is formed against me shall prosper'."

It only infuriated him.

Yet in this experience I felt total peace from the Comforter, the Holy Spirit. I remembered the statement, "You will be attacked, but not harmed."

The shooter emptied his revolver at me from a distance of about ten feet. I was untouched. My Helper, my *Paraklete*, my Comforter, was there.

Think about it!

With the power of the Holy Spirit, you can know the unknowable; you can see the unseeable; you can do the impossible. The Bible says to every believer, "nothing shall be impossible unto you" (Matthew 17:20, KJV).

THE HOLY SPIRIT OF TRUTH

John's Gospel gives the Holy Spirit another name: The Spirit of Truth.

> *"And I will pray the Father, and He will give you another Helper, that He may abide with you forever — the Spirit of truth, whom the world cannot receive, because it neither sees Him nor knows Him; but you know Him, for He dwells with you and will be in you."* (John 14:16–17, NKJV)

Truth is being rejected across America right now. Students are no longer reciting the Pledge of Allegiance in school. Professional athletes are refusing to stand in respect for the national anthem. Just as John's Gospel says, the world cannot accept God because it neither sees Him nor knows Him (see John 1:5, 10). But the truth is that we are still one nation under God. We are still endowed by our Creator with certain inalienable rights that include life, liberty, and the pursuit of happiness. Our dollar bills still declares, "In God we trust."

We are still the nation whose Founding Fathers answered the charge from Benjamin Franklin to pray as they wrote the constitution that would birth the United States of America.[83] We are still the nation whose sixteenth president, Abraham Lincoln, regularly called America to fasting and prayer, and who famously said, "I have been driven many times upon my knees by the overwhelming conviction that I had nowhere else to go."[84]

And who, in his second inaugural address, said to a nation at war with itself: "Fondly do we hope, fervently do we pray, that this mighty scourge of war may speedily pass away. Yet if God wills that it continues . . . until every drop of blood drawn with the lash shall be paid another drawn with the sword . . . so still it must be said that the judgments of the Lord are true and righteous altogether."[85]

When you live according to the Spirit, you walk in Truth, you walk in peace, you walk in freedom, life, and righteousness as a child of God and an heir to His promises (see Romans 8:1–17). Young people are crying in the streets, whining and complaining about what they are not getting. Oh entitled generation, I have one thing to say to you: Get a job! You are not slaves! You are free! You can do anything you want to do, so take your life and do something with it. That is the God-given truth. The truth, all truth, and nothing but the truth. So help me God.

The Spirit of truth not only speaks of things that were true in the past, or are true today, but also of things to come.

"When the Spirit of truth comes, he will guide you into all the truth, for he will not speak on his own authority, but whatever he hears he will speak, and he will declare to you the things that are to come." (John 16:13, ESV)

A headline appeared in May 1948 in the *San Antonio Light* that read: "Israel Reborn After 2,000 Years". What's so exciting about that? Ezekiel prophesied that this would happen . . . three thousand years ago! The Spirit of the Lord came to Ezekiel and told him to prophesy to the dry bones until flesh once again covered them, proclaiming that cities would be inhabited and ruins rebuilt, that Israel would once again dwell in the land given to her fathers. "You shall be My people, and I will be your God" (Ezekiel 36:28, NKJV).

Do we know the future? Absolutely! Because the Holy Spirit has revealed it to John the Revelator, to Daniel, to Ezekiel. When you put Daniel, Ezekiel, and Revelation together, you'll know more about tomorrow than *The Wall Street Journal*.

Ezekiel 36:35 says, "So they will say, 'This land that was desolate has become like the garden of Eden; and the wasted, desolate, and ruined cities are now fortified and inhabited'" (NKJV). You can go to Israel for yourself and see that the Jordan Valley looks like the Garden of Eden. How? Because the Spirit of God told Ezekiel,

> *"Behold, O My people, I will open your graves and*
> *cause you to come up from your graves, and bring*
> *you into the land of Israel. Then you shall know that*
> *I am the Lord, when I have opened your graves, O*
> *My people, and brought you up from your graves.*
> *I will put My Spirit in you, and you shall live, and*
> *I will place you in your own land. Then you shall*
> *know that I, the Lord, have spoken it and performed*
> *it," says the Lord.* (Ezekiel 37:12–14, NKJV)

Israel lives, in their own land, just as it was foretold by the Holy Spirit voice of prophecy.

> *And if the Spirit of him who raised Jesus from the*
> *dead is living in you, he who raised Christ from the*
> *dead will also give life to your mortal bodies because*
> *of his Spirit who lives in you.* (Romans 8:11, NIV)

When the trump of God has sounded and you have died, when you are in the grave and your body has decomposed to just ashes, the Holy Spirit will quicken your mortal body. Your body will be instantly recreated and reunited by the *BARA*, the creative power of God, and by the *RUACH*, the breath of God. Your body will instantly be joined to your spirit and sail into the heavens to meet the Lord.

How were our bodies created in the first place? Genesis 2:7 says, "God formed man of the dust of the ground" (KJV). If you're in the grave long enough, you will turn to dust. But when the trump of God sounds, the Holy Spirit responds to the breath of God and instantly you will become a living soul. When you die, the breath of God that transformed a lump of clay into the living body of Adam will transform your body in the grave and instantly you will rise on the Resurrection morning to meet the Lord in the air. Who does that? The Holy Spirit of God.

First Thessalonians 5:19–22 says, "Do not quench the Spirit. Do not despise prophecies. Test all things; hold fast what is good. Abstain from every form of evil" (NKJV). Not everyone who prophesies truly speaks for God. There are false prophets in the world. But that does not mean that the Holy Spirit voice of prophecy is not alive and well today. Don't stifle the Holy Spirit by assuming that all prophecies are from the devil. Test all things against the Scriptures, in community, and against the Spirit that lives in you. Hold fast to those that ring true.

Joel wrote:

"And it shall come to pass afterward that I will pour out My Spirit on all flesh; your sons and your

daughters shall prophesy, your old men shall dream dreams, your young men shall see visions. And also on My menservants and on My maidservants I will pour out My Spirit in those days." (Joel 2:28–29, NKJV)

God doesn't have a Holy Spirit sprinkle for you; He has an outpouring of the Holy Spirit as powerful as Niagara Falls. The outpouring of the Holy Spirit wasn't just a promise for the men of old; His Spirit is being poured out on you and your children and your children's children, from now until eternity. Jesus said, "And now I will send the Holy Spirit, just as my Father promised. But stay here in the city until the Holy Spirit comes and fills you with power from heaven" (Luke 24:49, NLT). The promise of the Father is a Holy Spirit downpour upon your life, filling you with the power to prophesy!

For prophecy never came by the will of man, but holy men of God spoke as they were moved by the Holy Spirit. (2 Peter 1:21, NKJV)

The men who wrote all the prophecies in the Bible didn't do so because they thought it was a neat idea. They wrote the prophecies because "they were moved by the Holy Spirit," the same spirit that lives in you. The Spirit of God is Truth and will lead you into all Truth and it's all right there in the Bible.

DIVINE LOVE

Do you know people who carry a fourteen-pound King James Bibles around but who are as mean as a two-headed snake? They are not Christians. They are just humans with big books. Romans 5:5 says, "Now hope does not disappoint, because the love of God has been poured out in our hearts by the Holy Spirit who was given to us" (Romans 5:5, NKJV). Love is the demonstration that you belong to God. Love is the hallmark of being a Christian. Love is a gift from the Holy Spirit.

Saint Paul wrote in the famous "love" chapter in the Bible:

> If I speak in the tongues of men or of angels, but do not have love, I am only a resounding gong or a clanging cymbal. If I have the gift of prophecy and can fathom all mysteries and all knowledge, and if I have a faith that can move mountains, but do not have love, I am nothing. If I give all I possess to the poor and give over my body to hardship that I may boast, but do not have love, I gain nothing. (1 Corinthians 13:1–3, NIV)

The gifts of the Spirit — prophecy, speaking in tongues, faith, charity, martyrdom — are nothing without the primary purpose of the Spirit: divine love. If you do not love the body of Christ, you sound like a noisy cowbell to God, and, contrary to popular TV, we do not need more cowbells. If you do not love your neighbor as yourself: you gain nothing; you are nothing; you do not have God in you; and you do not have the Holy Spirit.

Divine love is evidence of your salvation. Divine love is evidence that you really know the Lord. Divine love is evidence of the Holy Spirit on your life.

Dear friends, let us love one another, for love comes from God. Everyone who loves has been born of God and knows God. Whoever does not love does not know God, because God is love. (1 John 4:7–8, NIV)

God is love, and when you express that love in your life — that divine love that loves the unlovable, that loves the least of these, that loves even one's enemies — that is evidence that the Holy Spirit is at work in you.

WHAT'S IT WORTH

In Acts chapter 8, Simon the sorcerer saw that Peter and John were imparting the gift of the Holy Spirit onto people by the laying on of hands, so he inquired as to how much it would cost for him to acquire this same power. Peter assured him that the power of the Holy Spirit was not for sale:

*. . . "May your silver perish with you, because you thought you could obtain the gift of God with money! You have neither part nor lot in this matter, for your heart is not right before God. **Repent**, therefore, of this wickedness of yours, and **pray** to the Lord that, if possible, the intent of your heart may be forgiven you. For I see that you are in the gall of bitterness and in the bond of iniquity."* (Acts 8:20–23, ESV, emphasis added)

How can we open up to the power of the Holy Spirit and, through Him, receive all of these blessed promises? "Repent" and "pray," were the instructions that Peter gave to Simon. Not repent and PAY, repent and PRAY!

Likewise, on the day of Pentecost, Peter said to those who had just heard the Gospel in the Upper Room: "Repent, and let every one of you be baptized in the name of Jesus Christ for the remission of sins; and you shall receive the gift of the Holy Spirit" (Acts 2:38, NKJV).

Step one: repent. Step two: be baptized in water as a confession of sin. It's that simple. And then all of these benefits of the Holy Spirit are available to you.

The Holy Spirit hovers over you. The Holy Spirit enables you to be a witness to Christ. The Holy Spirit brings unity. The Holy Spirit is your Helper, allowing you to see the unseeable and know the unknowable. The Holy Spirit is the Spirit of truth that sets you free. The Holy Spirit is the voice of prophecy, the voice of prayer, the voice of love. The Holy Spirit quickens the dead and raises us to new life on Resurrection morning. That is the power of the Holy Spirit available to all who repent and are baptized as declared in the Word of God. And Holy Spirit power is priceless.

THE POWER OF THE BLOOD

"I am not a professional evangelist. I am a living piece of evidence that there is power in the blood of Jesus." –REINHARD BONNKE[86]

"I tell you the moment a man breaks away from this doctrine of blood, religion becomes a sham, because the whole teaching of this book is of one story, and this is, that Christ came into the world and died for our sins." –D.L. MOODY[87]

Forgive my blunt assessment, but our country is awash in blood — both real and make-believe. We're drowning in it. Let's begin with the make-believe variety.

Graphic violence and blood pour from our televisions and movie screens in quantities that would have made ruthless battlefield commanders like Alexander the Great and Genghis Khan recoil in disgust. Like the decadent Romans, we've turned bloodshed into entertainment. One perceptive cultural commentator wrote: "Our idea of amusement is watching our self-ordained heroes gallop over mountains of corpses, often employing the exact same brand of callous violence as the antagonists . . ."[88] But at least watching a movie is a passive exercise.

Video games now give impressionable young minds the opportunity to actively participate in mass carnage, as they shoot, slash, bludgeon, and dismember tens of thousands of people, all with immersive sight-and-sound realism. In fact, today's video games allow users to dial in the levels of realistic "blood-spatter and gore" their killings generate on the screen. And for even the youngest players, more is usually better.

Some have dared to ask what participating in thousands of blood-soaked virtual killings is doing to the minds of our young people. In response, the apologists for ultra-realistic video violence are quick to assure us that these games are harmless. That the act of pointing a virtual shotgun at a lifelike virtual opponent and pulling the trigger over and repeatedly and witnessing the grisly aftermath does nothing to warp the souls of our youth.

Our headlines testify to the contrary. We see mass murders in shopping centers. We weep to read of mad men, armed to the teeth, invading schools, laying waste to innocent children, and becoming national celebrities in the process. We shake our heads in sadness at the news reports of police officers ambushed and assassinated as they respond to false calls for assistance.

So accustomed and attracted to bloodshed have we become, that if every gun in America were to disappear tomorrow, the killing would continue unabated with knives, machetes, and rocks if necessary. Cars and trucks would become weapons. If you don't believe me, ask the citizens of Israel or London.

These are only the visible, publicized bloodlettings. A vast, largely unseen holocaust has been taking place on our shores for more than four decades. Behind the closed doors of America's abortion clinics, millions upon millions of innocents have been sacrificed to the gods of convenience and leftist ideologies. By conservative estimates, the toll is more than sixty million and rising since 1973's Roe v. Wade decision.[89]

One of the most recent rationales trotted out to justify the continued killing of the preborn is defense of the environment. The modern, "enlightened" view is that humans are a plague upon this planet. A destructive virus. A cancer that must be cut out. Rather than embracing God's declaration in Genesis that we're made in the image and likeness of Him, and that He has granted us divine stewardship authority over this beautiful earth, we're told that we don't belong here. Thus, any measures that reduce the future population should be enthusiastically embraced, we're told.

Think about that for a moment. In a sense, there are many among us who would return us to the practice of primitive pagans of ancient times — sacrificing infants to appease angry weather gods.

If the blood of innocent Abel cried out from the ground, oh, what a multitude of voices must cry out to God from the soil of America the Beautiful in our day! The prophet Isaiah once thundered God's indictment of another society that, like ours, had tossed away its moral compass:

> . . . *Thus He looked for justice, but behold,*
> *bloodshed; for righteousness, but behold,*
> *a cry of distress.* (Isaiah 5:7, NASB)

God is still looking for justice among the societies of men. And He still finds bloodshed — particularly that of the helpless and the innocent — an abomination. Proverbs, the Bible's wisdom book, reveals that "hands that shed innocent blood" is among the six things that God hates (Proverbs 6:17, NASB).

This presents a vital question: What is it about blood that makes it so precious to God, and makes His sworn enemy so determined to spill it?

LIFE IS IN THE BLOOD

There is indeed something precious about blood. Something sacred. It's impossible to read your Bible without drawing that conclusion. The headwaters of God's crimson stream of redemption lie on the opening pages of your Bible. In the early chapters of Genesis, God Himself appears with animal skins from freshly slaughtered animals to cover the shame of the man and woman — who He had created to be the crowning achievement of His six days of creative activity. We find it in the final book of the Bible, where the hosts of heaven sing glorious songs of the slain, "worthy" Lamb:

> *And they sang a new song, saying, "Worthy are you to take the scroll and to open its seals, for you were slain, and by your blood you ransomed people for God from every tribe and language and people and nation."* (Revelation 5:9, ESV)

There, too, in Revelation, the blood of martyred saints cries out for justice from beneath the altar in heaven's holy courtroom:

And when he had opened the fifth seal, I saw under the altar the souls of them that were slain for the word of God, and for the testimony which they held: And they cried with a loud voice, saying, How long, O Lord, holy and true, dost thou not judge and avenge our blood on them that dwell on the earth? (Revelation 6:9–10, KJV)

We find the significance of blood everywhere in between Genesis and Revelation in the Word of God. For example, in explaining the Mosaic covenant's sacrificial system to Moses, God Himself declares:

For the life of the flesh is in the blood: and I have given it to you upon the altar to make an atonement for your souls: for it is the blood that maketh an atonement for the soul. (Leviticus 17:11, KJV)

Clearly, even the blood of bulls and goats has sacred value because it represents the miracle of life. But on the pages that follow, you'll come to appreciate just how precious and how indescribably powerful is the blood of the innocent Lamb of God, who takes away the sin of the world.

Of course, we live in a generation that worships power. We celebrate athletes and teams that display it. Our movies exalt characters who wield it. Wall Street's self-styled "masters of the universe" trade their very souls in a quest to grasp it. The world's military forces enlist their nation's greatest minds in an endless race to develop ever-more-destructive weapon systems. More than anything else, what we want from our cars, our computers, and our vitamin supplements is "more power."

How ironic, then, that our power-obsessed culture has largely overlooked or dismissed the most potent, transformative substance ever to exist — the blood of Jesus Christ.

Do you know what blood type Jesus is? He is O negative. He is the universal donor, and His blood is unlimited. He doesn't have to wait fifty-six days until He can give blood again. Just as our blood supply replenishes itself, the blood of Christ is for eternity.

Moses writes, "the life of the flesh is in the blood" (Leviticus 17:11, KJV).

The only part of our anatomy that can move throughout the body is the blood. In less than sixty seconds, the blood will circulate from the heart, through the entire body, and back again. It carries oxygen and nutrients and cleansing power. It is literally life giving.

"If we confess our sins, He is faithful and just to forgive us *our* sins and to cleanse us from all unrighteousness" (1 John 1:9, NKJV). The blood not only gives life but cleanses us from all impurities.

Some day you will get to the point where a doctor will grab you by the hand and check your wrist for a pulse that is created by moving blood. But if the blood isn't moving, neither are you!

In the same way that a bloodless body is a dead body, a bloodless theology is a dead theology. Without the doctrine of atonement, Christianity is the doctrine of demons. It's another Gospel. Paul writes viciously about another Gospel.

A bloodless church is a dead church. You can have all the lights and cameras and fancy screens and smoke machines you want, but if you don't have the testimony of the blood of Jesus Christ, you are nothing but sounding brass and a tinkling cymbal.

A bloodless prayer is a dead prayer. You can have all the crystals and visualization and meditation and positive thinking you want, but if you don't have the blood of the testimony, demons will laugh your prayers right out of heaven. You can go to hell feeling good about yourself, because it takes the power of the blood to enter heaven's gates.

When the blood circulates, it connects every part of the body. The blood of Jesus Christ connects every member of the Church into one body, the body of Christ.

I once heard two grown men arguing over baptism and how long a person needed to stay under water in order to be saved, as if spending the night in the baptistery would make you "more baptized" than one dunk, or two, or three. Jesus groans and God just shakes His head when man gets to arguing over the doctrine and procedure of baptism.

The God-given truth of the matter is that there is one Lord, one baptism, one Savior, one Bible. When you come to the foot of the cross, you are one in the family of God.

Denominations divide us; the blood unifies us. Doctrines divide us; the blood unifies us. Racial issues divide us; the blood unifies us. Politics divide us; the blood unifies us.

That precious crimson cascade represents the most awesome power God Almighty has ever released on planet earth. Indeed, Satan's greatest fear is that God's people will rediscover and proclaim the wonder-working power of the precious blood of the Lamb of God that takes away the sins of the world.

That blood is the secret of unlimited power in our preaching and our praying. It is the blood of Jesus Christ that makes the Word of God immutable and irresistible. It strikes terror into the heart of every demon in hell. It shatters the chains that bind the captives and sets them gloriously free. Let's explore why.

THE PRINCIPLE OF BLOOD ATONEMENT

At the moment of creation, God wove certain principles and truths into the very fabric of the universe. Among these is the principle that the redemption of the guilty requires the suffering and death of an innocent.

Numerous scriptures either hint at this or state it explicitly. It is with good reason that God had the Israelites foreshadow and depict the future sacrifice of His only begotten Son by having them sacrifice a spotless, unblemished lamb.

Hebrews 9:22 proclaims this eternal truth in clear language: "And according to the law almost all things are purified with blood, and without shedding of blood there is no remission" (NKJV). No blood; no forgiveness. God isn't messing around. He speaks plainly because He wants you to plainly see: there is power in the blood.

In the third chapter of Romans, Paul declares this truth as well, but in language that may be unfamiliar to many modern ears:

> Being justified freely by his grace through the redemption that is in Christ Jesus: Whom God hath set forth to be a propitiation through faith in his blood, to declare his righteousness for the remission of sins that are past, through the forbearance of God. (Romans 3:24–25, KJV)

Propitiation isn't a word we hear much these days, but it describes an offering that restores the favor and blessing of the King. It is an appropriate and worthy payment that restores relationship and connection. Peter points out that gold and silver lose their value, but the blood of the sinless, spotless Lamb is forever (see 1 Peter 1:18–19).

The Greek word *hilasterion*, from which propitiation is translated, points clearly to the Mercy Seat — the lid of the Ark of the Covenant — within the Holy of Holies in the Tabernacle of Moses. Here, and throughout the Word of God, we see that Jesus's blood was not only sufficient to remit the sins of all mankind, but it was absolutely necessary! Without the shedding of innocent blood, there can be no remission of sin.

It is no accident that God commanded the captive Israelites to paint the doorposts of their homes with the blood of an unblemished male lamb. The blood of the male lamb sprinkled over the door, on the sides of the door, in the trough, at the base of the door, and over the top of the door of the house declared that the house was sealed by the Lamb's blood.

When the death angel came through Egypt, everyone who had blood over the door was spared. And everyone who did not, the firstborn in their family died that night. Tears were heard from one end of Egypt to the other. But from the houses where there was blood over the doorposts, there was nothing but peace and tranquility. God was in the process of restoring His chosen people to their rightful place, rescuing them from slavery and bringing them back to the land that He had promised them.

The blood of the firstborn was as necessary for the Israelites as it was for the Egyptians, but that precious blood would come from one Son, the Son of God, to seal the house of all who proclaimed the Lord as their Savior.

The blood is our protection. The blood is our power. The blood is our Passover. The Old Testament blood was necessary for every divine right, for the consecration of the house, for the birth of a child, for repentance of sin, for festivals, for blood-covenant contracts. God Almighty made a blood covenant contract in Genesis 17 to the Jewish people, to Abraham, Isaac, and Jacob, and to their descendants for the land of Israel. A blood covenant was made that can never be broken, based on the integrity of God, that the land of Israel does in its totality belong to the Jewish people. That's not just in the past, that's for today, and for 10,000 years into the future, because God said so; so, it is settled.

In the first chapter of John, John the Baptist declares, "Behold! The Lamb of God who takes away the sin of the world!" (John 1:29, NKJV). John's job was to pave the way for the coming Messiah, and the first words he says when he sees Jesus are a declaration of what is to come: Jesus's purpose was to be killed. He was the spotless male lamb. He was without blemish. He was holy. He was pure. He was destined to die from the foundations of the world. He was the only perfect Man to ever live, and yet His purpose was to carry our sins — yours and mine — to the cross and leave them there, never to be remembered any more.

In ancient Israel, a goat was taken to the edge of a mountain, where the sins of the people were symbolically placed on its head. The goat was thrown over the edge of the cliff, and upon its death, so were the sins of Israel forgiven. This is the source of the word "scapegoat."

Jesus was our scapegoat. Yet, unlike the actual goat who only covered the people's sins for a year, Jesus carried our sins "once and for all" (see Romans 6:10). The blood of Jesus was the ultimate and last sacrifice, and the transfer of power from death to life.

At Calvary, the lamb was slain. The scarlet stream of blood trickled down that old, rugged cross and onto the pages of Acts, Romans, Corinthians, Galatians, Ephesians, Philippians, Colossians, Thessalonians, Timothy, Titus, Philemon, Hebrews, First and Second Peter, First and Second and Third John, Jude, and Revelation:

> *. . . and from Jesus Christ, the faithful witness, the firstborn from the dead, and the ruler over the kings of the earth. To Him who loved us and washed us from our sins in His own blood, and has made us kings and priests*

to His God and Father, to Him be glory and dominion
forever and ever. Amen. (Revelation 1:5–6, NKJV)

The precious blood shed on the Cross is not to be confused with the blood of the first plague in Egypt. The precious blood is not to be confused with the blood of the
22,000 oxen and 120,000 sheep that Solomon slaughtered
when he dedicated the temple. The precious blood is not
to be confused with the blood of innocent children shed
by Herod, who sought to kill the baby Jesus by ordering
the mass murder of all children born in that timeframe.

The precious blood is not to be confused with the
blood of the early Christians who were martyred for their
faith. The only blood that can remove the crimson stain
of sin from your soul is the precious blood of the Lamb
of God for sinner's slain, the blood of Emmanuel that
cleanses us from all unrighteousness and terrifies every
demon in hell. His. Own. Blood.

THE POWER OF CHRIST'S SACRIFICE

The blood of Jesus Christ shed for your redemption and
for mine will never lose its power.

Like men drag an ox to be slaughtered, Jesus was
dragged from His place of prayer in Gethsemane to a
place of agony. In merciless mockery, a purple robe was
placed upon His shoulders. In unmatched cruelty, a

crown of thorns was thrust upon His head. On Creation morning, God the Father, God the Son, and God the Holy Spirit created man, and now the created was destroying the Creator.

Jesus had so much power. With one word, He could have pulverized the earth and destroyed every human being, yet He used His strength to remain silent. He allowed His own murder so that you and I would know, beyond the shadow of a doubt, that our sins have been buried in the deepest sea, never to be remembered against us anymore. We are the Church triumphant. We are whiter than snow. We are free.

Brutally beaten, Jesus was forced to walk to His own death while another man carried His cross. On a hill called Golgotha, Roman soldiers nailed Jesus's hands and feet to His execution pole and raised Him up to be mocked by everyone traveling the busy thoroughfare. The soldiers made a game of it, gambling for His clothes.

Even after Jesus had taken His last breath, His body continued to be brutalized. Because He was already dead, the soldiers did not break His legs like they did to the two men crucified beside Him, Instead, one of the soldiers pierced Jesus's side with a spear, bringing a sudden flow of blood and water (see John 19:34). Dwight L. Moody remarked:

Look at that Roman soldier as he pushed his spear into the very heart of the God-man. What a hellish deed! But what was the next thing that took place? Blood covered the spear! Oh! Thank God, the blood covers sin. There was the blood covering that spear — the very point of it. The very crowning act of sin brought out the crowning act of love; the crowning act of wickedness was the crowning act of grace.[90]

William Cowper wrote the familiar hymn, "There is a Fountain Filled with Blood." Most of us know the first verse, yet all the lyrics are timeless:

There is a fountain filled with blood
Drawn from Immanuel's veins;
And sinners, plunged beneath that flood,
Lose all their guilty stains;
And sinners, plunged beneath that flood,
Lose all their guilty stains.

The dying thief rejoiced to see
That fountain in his day;
And there may I, though vile as he,
Wash all my sins away;
And there may I, though vile as he,
Wash all my sins away.

Dear dying Lamb,
Thy precious blood
Shall never lose its power,
Till all the ransomed ones of God,
Be saved, to sin no more;
Till all the ransomed ones of God,
Be saved, to sin no more.

E'er since by faith I saw the stream
Thy flowing wounds supply,
Redeeming love has been my theme, and shall be till I die;
Redeeming love has been my theme,
And shall be till I die.

When this poor lisping, stammering tongue
Lies silent in the grave,
Then in a nobler, sweeter song,
I'll sing Thy power to save;
Then in a nobler, sweeter song,
I'll sing Thy power to save.[91]

The "power to save!" Without the blood, there is no hope. Without the blood, there is no future. Without the blood, there is no power. WITH the blood, we have everlasting life and victory over death, hell, and the grave.

The tomb of Joseph of Arimathea, where Jesus was laid after the crucifixion, is empty. He is not there! The angels removed the stone, not to let Jesus out, but to let us in so that we could see that God accepted the sacrifice. And because He lives, we shall also live.

Consider what we have through the blood of Jesus. We have unlimited power for protection. When I die and my body leaves this earth, angels are going to carry me through the second heaven, which is the devil's bedroom. The devil is going to see me coming and He's going to say to every power and principality: "Back up! Don't touch! He's covered with the blood of the lamb, and He's on the way to the Father's throne."

Without the blood of Jesus Christ, Christianity is a powerless fraud. Without the blood of Jesus Christ, the Church is a religious fraternity of people living in absolute deception. Without the blood of Jesus Christ, our preaching is in vain, our worship is a farce. Without the blood: we have ritual without righteousness, ceremony without conversion, and deception without discipleship. Without the blood of Jesus Christ, the Church is nothing because it has nothing to offer if it doesn't offer salvation for the soul.

You are saved by the blood, washed by the blood of the One Jesus Christ. It is only the blood that can remove the death penalty from my life and from yours: "Christ hath redeemed us from the curse of the law" (Galatians 3:13, KJV). He became the curse for us, and that curse was broken when He said, "It is finished" (John 19:30, NKJV).

It is not possible for you to get to heaven until you accept the substitutionary death of Jesus Christ on the cross as your Redeemer. If you do not accept His death, you are required to pay for your sins, and trust me, you don't have enough buying power to purchase your redemption into heaven.

THE SIGNIFICANCE OF COMMUNION

Symbolically, Communion is a blood transfusion from the throne of God. According to the Red Cross, someone in the United States needs blood every two seconds.[92] One man's donation has the potential to save three lives, but Jesus's blood has the potential to save the world.

Speaking to the disciples at the final communion service, Jesus said, "For this is My blood of the new covenant, which is shed *for many* for the remission of sins" (Matthew 26:28, NKJV, emphasis added).

You are part of that "many." Communion is a celebration of blood shed for you, for your redemption.

Jesus said, this is my blood of the new covenant, drink all of it and life will be yours for all eternity:

Then Jesus said to them, "Most assuredly, I say to you, unless you eat the flesh of the Son of Man and drink His blood, you have no life in you. Whoever eats My flesh and drinks My blood has eternal life, and I will

*raise him up at the last day. For My flesh is food indeed,
and My blood is drink indeed. He who eats My flesh
and drinks My blood abides in Me, and I in him. As the
living Father sent Me, and I live because of the Father,
so he who feeds on Me will live because of Me. This is
the bread which came down from heaven — not as
your fathers ate the manna, and are dead. He who eats
this bread will live forever.*" (John 6:53–58, NKJV)

Sin is like a virus in your blood, and the only solution is a blood transfusion. When we lift the Communion cup to our lips, we're symbolically taking in the supernatural, life-changing blood of Jesus Christ that drives that virus out. Blood not only carries oxygen to the body, but it also eliminates waste products that the body creates. Likewise, the blood of Jesus not only gives life, but cleanses us from all unrighteousness (see 1 John 1:9).

*When we bless the cup at the Lord's Table, aren't
we sharing in the blood of Christ? And when
we break the bread, aren't we sharing in the
body of Christ?* (1 Corinthians 10:16, NLT)

When you take the Holy Communion, Satan sobs. He knows he has lost you. He knows you are safe, untouchable, covered with the blood of Jesus, a shield of protection around you. Paul wrote in his letter to the Ephesians:

"But now in Christ Jesus ye who sometimes were far off are made nigh by the blood of Christ" (Ephesians 2:13, KJV). "Made nigh" means to be brought near.

Paul was saying to the Gentile believers: "You used to be outsiders. You didn't know God. You didn't know His power or His promises to all who believe." But the blood of Christ isn't just for Jews. It's also for Gentiles. Satan no longer has a hold on you. He can't come near you. Welcome to the family!

Communion is not a get-out-of-jail-free card, however. Communion taken unworthily will send you to the grave. Listen to what Paul has to say to the Corinthian church:

For I received from the Lord that which I also delivered to you: that the Lord Jesus on the same night in which He was betrayed took bread; and when He had given thanks, He broke it and said, "Take, eat; this is My body which is broken for you; do this in remembrance of Me." In the same manner He also took the cup after supper, saying, "This cup is the new covenant in My blood. This do, as often as you drink it, in remembrance of Me." For as often as you eat this bread and drink this cup, you proclaim the Lord's death till He comes. Therefore whoever eats this bread or drinks this cup of the Lord in an unworthy manner will be guilty of the body and blood of the Lord. But let a man examine himself, and so let him eat of the bread and drink of the cup. For he who eats and drinks in an unworthy manner eats and drinks judgment to himself, not discerning the Lord's body. For this reason many are weak and sick among you, and many sleep. For if we would judge ourselves, we would not be judged. But when we are judged, we are chastened by the Lord, that we may not be condemned with the world. Therefore, my brethren, when you come together to eat, wait for one another. But if anyone is hungry, let him eat at home, lest you come together for judgment. And the rest I will set in order when I come. (1 Corinthians 11:23–34, NKJV)

Essentially, what Paul is saying is that if you take the Holy Communion without confession and with known sin in your life, you are making a mockery of what Jesus did for you. And God won't stand for that. Just look at Adam and Eve if you don't believe me. God didn't kick them out of Eden because they sinned, but because they refused to confess their sin.

From Eden to eternity, confession is and has always been the key to receiving the power that is yours when God freely hands you the keys to the kingdom. The blood of Jesus is not "a common thing" (Hebrews 10:29, NKJV): it is holy; it is sanctified; it brings mercy and grace. Therefore, communion is to be taken in a worthy manner as a remembrance of who Jesus was, is, and is to come, and all that He has done for you.

THE IMPLICATIONS OF THE BLOOD

Little Johnny wasn't very bright. In fact, he was failing fifth grade math. His parents blamed the public-school system, so they pulled him out and enrolled him in a private Catholic school. After his first day of Catholic school, little Johnny came home and ran straight to his room and locked the door. He came out for a quick dinner, then announced he had to go back to his room and study. This pattern continued for the entire semester. At the end of the term, little Johnny brought home his report card. His parents cautiously opened the report card and saw a capital "A" under the subject math. "Was it the nuns?" his father asked. Little Johnny shook his head no.

"Was it the teacher?" his mother asked. Again, Johnny shook his head no. Johnny's parents kept trying: "Was it the tutoring? Your classmates? The curriculum?" Finally, Johnny spoke up: "From the very first day of school, I knew these folks were serious about math. When I walked into the office and saw a guy nailed to a plus sign, I knew they meant business."[93]

The blood of Jesus, shed for your sins, is serious business. Satan's greatest fear is the blood of Jesus Christ. The secret of unlimited power in our preaching, in our praying, in our praising, is the precious blood of Jesus Christ. It is the blood that makes the Word of God powerful. It terrorizes Satan and every demon in hell. It sets the captives free from the chains that enslave them. It is the blood that guarantees my salvation and yours. It is the blood that conquers death, hell, and the grave. It is the blood that brings healing: "and with his stripes we are healed" (Isaiah 53:5, KJV).

It is the blood that breaks generational curses. In the early chapters of Joshua, Moses had just died, and Joshua stepped up to take his place as shepherd to the Israelites. Joshua sent out two young men to spy out the land, especially Jericho, as the Israelites prepared to enter the Promised Land after 40 years in the wilderness. The young men ended up at the house of a harlot named Rahab. Rahab hid the two men from her community because she feared the Lord.

In exchange for protecting them, she asked the men to spare her family when the Israelites returned to take Jericho. The men told her to place a scarlet cord in her window so that they would know to pass over the household and everyone in it. When the Israelites saw the scarlet cord, they kept their promise and spared Rahab and her family before burning Jericho to the ground.

Rahab, the harlot, saved her family. Rahab, the harlot, became a believer. Rahab, the harlot, is named in the lineage of Christ (see Matthew 1:5). Like Rahab, you need to draw the blood circle around your family and let your family be protected by the blood of Jesus Christ.

The scarlet cord was to Rahab what the blood-smeared doorposts were to the Israelites. In Exodus 12, on the night when God passed through Egypt, He kept the promise He had made to the children of Israel: "And the blood shall be to you for a token upon the houses where ye are: and when I see the blood, I will pass over you, and the plague shall not be upon you to destroy you, when I smite the land of Egypt" (Exodus 12:13, KJV).

It wasn't rubies or diamonds on their doorposts that saved them. It wasn't the golden rule or a large offering. It wasn't idols made of silver or gold or bronze. The death angel passed over only those houses that had been washed in the blood.

The scarlet cord, the blood-smeared doorposts, the crimson blood upon the cross. One drop of that precious blood sets you free from the bondage of sin: ". . . though your sins be as scarlet, they shall be as white as snow; though they be red like crimson, they shall be as wool" (Isaiah 1:18, KJV). God can no more remember a sin that has been forgiven by the blood of Jesus Christ than you can uncover buried treasure that has been lost at sea.

If you don't believe that, let me ask you this: Who was the first person to get to heaven by the blood of Jesus Christ? A career criminal. One of the two men who were crucified alongside Jesus. This criminal made his confession of guilt on the cross, declaring that he was being "punished justly" (Luke 23:41, NIV) for his wrongdoing, then asked Jesus to remember him. And Jesus replied, "Assuredly, I say to you, today you will be with Me in Paradise" (Luke 23:43, NKJV). Heaven's gates! Jesus takes everybody! That is the power of the blood!

One drop of blood and God made His peace with everything that is in the world and in heaven. One drop of blood from the Lamb of God and the angels write your name in the Lamb's Book of Life. One drop of the power of the blood and your chains are broken. You are adopted as a child of the King. You are loved. You are royalty. You are family. You are destined to wear the crown of life and a robe of righteousness while you lounge around at home in your mansion built by the Architect of the Ages.

The blood of Jesus Christ is the only way to salvation. Secular humanists say, "We're all on different roads going to the same place." There is not a verse in Scripture to support that. Without the shedding of blood, there is no remission of sins. That is God's law.

If crocodile tears could save us, every actress in Hollywood would be Mother Teresa.

If good deeds could save us, Jesus died for no reason.

If financial gifts could save us, Jesus would not have said it was easier to thread the eye of a needle with a camel than for a rich man to enter heaven (see Matthew 19:24).

The Bible is clear: without the shedding of blood, there is no remission of sin.

Random acts of kindness cannot save you. Church membership cannot save you. Baptism cannot save you. Without the blood of Jesus, you'll go into the baptismal font a dry sinner and come up a wet one. The blood of turtle doves cannot save you. A river of blood from bulls and goats could never save you. Only the precious blood of the spotless Lamb of God can save you! There is power in the blood.

> *And Jesus Christ was revealed as God's Son by his baptism in water and by shedding his blood on the cross — not by water only, but by water and blood. And the Spirit, who is truth, confirms it with his testimony. So we have these three witnesses — the Spirit, the water, and the blood — and all three agree.* (1 John 5:6–8, NLT)

There is pow'r, pow'r, wonder-working pow'r in the precious blood of the Lamb.[94]

CONCLUSION

We are living in a historic moment in which seemingly everything that can be shaken is being shaken. Oh, how we need heavenly power in this hour.

The greatest need in America is to see the power of the Lord manifest in the Church. We need to be conduits of that power. Carriers of that power. Releasers of that power of God.

It is appropriate that we do so. The kingdom of God came with power. The Lord's Prayer asks us to pray for kingdom and power and glory. Acts 2 says, "you shall receive power" (NKJV). Luke 9 says, "I give you power" (NKJV). Revelation 2:27 says to rule with power. Paul said to the Corinthians, "For the Kingdom of God is not just a lot of talk; it is living by God's power" (1 Corinthians 4:20, NLT). The supernatural power of God is necessary, and it is available to every blood-washed child of God who is willing to receive it and release it. Paul made it his mission statement.

> *For I am not ashamed of the gospel of Christ:*
> *for it is the power of God unto salvation to*
> *every one that believeth; to the Jew first, and*
> *also to the Greek.* (Romans 1:16, KJV)

Are we slumbering at the switch at this most dangerous hour? A revolution begins with the preaching of God's power to the New Testament Church and activating that power in our lives and our churches and our world.

> *I also pray that you will understand the incredible*
> *greatness of God's power for us who believe him. This*
> *is the same mighty power that raised Christ from the*
> *dead and seated him in the place of honor at God's*
> *right hand in the heavenly realms. Now he is far above*
> *any ruler or authority or power or leader or anything*
> *else — not only in this world but also in the world to*
> *come. God has put all things under the authority of*
> *Christ and has made him head over all things for the*
> *benefit of the church. And the church is his body; it is*

made full and complete by Christ, who fills all things everywhere with himself. (Ephesians 1:19–23, NLT)

Prayer is the secret to releasing the supernatural power of God in your life, your marriage, your business, your finances, your mind, and your church. If there was only one verse in the Bible that you could believe and it would change your life forever it would be this one: "Therefore I tell you, whatever you ask for in prayer, believe that you have received it, and it will be yours" (Mark 11:24, NIV). John says it this way: "If you abide in Me, and My words abide in you, you will ask what you desire, and it shall be done for you" (John 15:7, NKJV). As a child of God, you have the right to receive whatever you ask.

If a very rich man walked in here and gave you a blank check and said you could use it any time, for the rest of your life, for any amount, you would believe for great things. God Almighty, whose streets are paved with pure gold, handed you a blank check when He said all you have to do is ask, and when you believe the check is real, all that you ask for is yours to have.

In John 14:12, Jesus said, "Very truly I tell you, whoever believes in me will do the works I have been doing, and they will do even greater things than these, because I am going to the Father" (NIV).

Jesus didn't mean greater things in quality, but greater things in quantity or number. Jesus was only one person.

He was the limiting factor. But the Holy Spirit is now in every person who has received God, therefore the power of God to do the works that Jesus did is within each one of us who are in the family of faith.

Every person reading these words right now who has prayed and received the Holy Spirit has that kind of power. So, when He put God, the Holy Spirit, in you, He gave you the ability to put your hand on the head of a sick person and command that sickness to go away. He gave you the ability to bring the forces of hell into subjection. The devil is afraid of you! God in you is the power to do whatever God says you can do and have whatever God says you can have — hope, wealth, forgiveness, success in relationships and everything that your hand touches, and peace and joy in this life and the one to come. That is the power that Jesus died for you to have!

When I think of all this, I fall to my knees and pray to the Father, the Creator of everything in heaven and on earth. I pray that from his glorious, unlimited resources he will empower you with inner strength through his Spirit. Then Christ will make his home in your hearts as you trust in him. Your roots will grow down into God's love and keep you strong. And may you have the power to understand, as all God's people should, how wide, how long, how high, and how deep his love is. May you experience the love of Christ, though it is too great to understand fully. Then you will be made complete with all the fullness of life and power that comes from God. Now all glory to God, who is able, through his mighty power at work within us, to accomplish infinitely more than we might ask or think. Glory to him in the church and in Christ Jesus through all generations forever and ever! Amen. (Ephesians 3:14–21, NLT)

Dear Saint, from this day forward . . . may you live a life characterized by His Absolute Power.

ENDNOTES

1. Wolf, Katherine and Jay, *Hope Heals*, Zondervan: Grand Rapids, MI, 2016.

2. https://jewishweek.timesofisrael.com/the-plague-was-more-than-blood/

3. https://www.goodreads.com/quotes/7454768-supernatural-hope-is-the-virtue-that-strips-us-of-all.

4. *Illustrations Unlimited*, Tyndale House Publishers, Wheaton, Illinois, pp. 291-292.

5. *Illustrations Unlimited*; Tyndale House Publishers, Wheaton, Illinois, pp. 289-290.

6. Jungreis, Rebbetzin Esther. *The Committed Life*, Harper Collins, 1998, pp. 186-187.

7. https://www.psychologytoday.com/us/blog/the-asymmetric-brain/201812/3-surprising-ways-hugging-benefits-your-well-being

8. https://www.census.gov/newsroom/press-releases/2016/cb16-192.html

9. Dubin, Burt. *Chicken Soup for the Soul*, Chicken Soup for the Soul Publishing, LLC, pp. 298-299.

10. Source: Peale, Norman Vincent, *The Power of Positive Thinking*, Fawcett, 1992, p. 51

11. Source: Sweatt, Lydia, *15 Quotes to Inspire You to Reach Your Greatest Potential*; April 20, 2017, https://www.success.com/15-quotes-to-inspire-you-to-reach-your-greatest-potential/

12. Source: Washington, Booker T., *My Larger Education*, Garden City New York, Doubleday, 1911, pp. 4-6. https://docsouth.unc.edu/fpn/washeducation/washing.html

13. Source: http://www.lifewithoutlimbs.org/about-nick/bio/

14. Source: https://www.joniandfriends.org/about/our-history/

15. Source: https://www.scientificamerican.com/article/do-people-only-use-10-percent-of-their-brains/

16. Source: https://www.livescience.com/53751-brain-could-store-internet.html

17. Source: http://www.cnn.com/2009/TECH/06/10/million.words/index.html

18. Source: https://www.pewforum.org/2015/05/12/americas-changing-religious-landscape/

19. Source: Kuzma, Kay, *Family Times*, Vol. 1, No. 3, Fall 1992, p. 1. http://www.sermonillustrations.com/a-z/p/parenting.htm

20. Source: https://www.telegraph.co.uk/news/religion/10458380/Christianity-at-risk-of-dying-out-in-a-generation-warns-Lord-Carey.html

21. Source: Jackie Green, Lauren Green McAfee, Bill High, "Only One Life" (2018), Zondervan, Grand Rapids, MI.

22. Source: *Today in the Word*, February 1991, p. 33. http://www.sermonillustrations.com/a-z/p/potential.htm

23. Source: https://www.irvingberlin.com/biography

24. Source: *Today in the Word*, December 3, 1992. http://www.sermonillustrations.com/a-z/p/potential.htm

25. Source: Sweatt, Lydia, *15 Quotes to Inspire You to Reach Your Greatest Potential*; April 20, 2017, https://www.success.com/15-quotes-to-inspire-you-to-reach-your-greatest-potential/

26. Source: Unknown. http://www.sermonillustrations.com/a-z/p/parenting.htm

27. Wiesenthal, Simon. *The Sunflower*. Schocken Books Inc.: New York, 1998.

28. Smedes, Lewis. *Forgive and Forget*. Harper & Row, 1984.

29. Jett, Phllip. *The Death of an Heir*. St. Martin's Press: New York, 2017.

30. http://drjamesdobson.org, Dr. James Dobson's Family Talk, "A Visit with the Coors Part 1 and 2"

31. https://www.ministrymagazine.org/archive/1963/07/forgiveness-in-the-new-testament

32. Laurie, Greg "Forgiveness Is Not Optional." *harvest.org*.

33. https://www.nytimes.com/2013/12/06/world/africa/nelson-mandela_obit.html

34. http://www.elisabethelliot.org/about.html

35. https://www.npr.org/templates/story/story.php?storyId=14900930

36. ten Boom, Corrie with Jamie Buckingham. *Tramp for the Lord*. Jove Books: New York, 1978, p. 55. (Originally published in Guideposts Magazine, 1972.)

37. de Jong, Paul. *God, Money & Me*. Life Resource International: New Zealand, 2017.

38. https://www.azquotes.com/quote/552298. Quoted in Peter Collier and David Horowitz, *The Rockefellers, an American Dynasty*, 1976.

39. Eds. Applewhite, Ashton; Evans III, William R; Frothingham, Andrew; *And I Quote* (Revised Edition), St. Martin's Press: New York, (2003) p. xiv.

40. https://www.azquotes.com/quote/1424951. Calvin, John. *Commentary on Luke*. Ravenio Books, 2013, p.389.

41. https://www.christianity.com/church/church-history/timeline/1901-2000/jc-penney-11630672.html

42. https://nextgenerationstewardship.wordpress.com/2008/08/18/soap-and-toothpaste-a-testimony-about-giving/. Quoted from G. Ernest Thomas, *Spiritual Life through Tithing* (1953).

43. https://youtube/g2hgWFuJyv8

44. https://www.forbes.com/sites/erikaandersen/2013/12/02/23-quotes-from-warren-buffett-on-life-and-generosity/#8a4f306f891b

45. https://pushpay.com/blog/church-giving-statistics/

46. https://www.sermoncentral.com/sermon-illustrations/80884/a-man-once-came-to-peter-marshall-former-by-josh-hunt

47. Gray, John. *Men Are From Mars, Women Are From Venus*. Harper Collins, 1992.

48. https://www.wiseoldsayings.com/communication-quotes/#ixzz6OmUu5DXj

49. https://www.google.com/search?q=communication&rlz=1C5CHFA_enUS905US905&oq=communication&aqs=chrome..69i57j0l6j69i60.5863j1j7&sourceid=chrome&ie=UTF-8

50. https://www.sermoncentral.com/sermons/communication-or-miscommunication-dean-courtier-sermon-on-action-151388

51. https://nypost.com/2018/03/20/american-families-barely-spend-quality-time-together/

52. https://www.heraldsun.com.au/subscribe/news/1/?sourceCode=HSWEB_WRE170_a&dest=https%3A%2F%2Fwww.heraldsun.com.au%2Fnews%2Ffathers-spend-less-than-20-seconds-a-day-talking-to-teen-sons-leading-educator-warns%2Fnews-story%2F35e68b6a4f9c7f6951acdf924a42e130&memtype=anonymous&mode=premium

53. https://www.biomat.com/hands-feet-and-reflexology-the-gateways-to-total-body-health/

54. https://www.kindspring.org/story/view.php?sid=7854

55. http://itre.cis.upenn.edu/~myl/languagelog/archives/003420.html

56. Maxwell, John C. *Everyone Communicates, Few Connect*. Thomas Nelson, 2010.

57. https://www.wiseoldsayings.com/communication-quotes/#ixzz6OmSy7Zhs

58. http://appleseeds.org/Waitley_Children.htm

59. Tozer, A. W. *How to Be Filled With The Holy Spirit*, 1952.

60. Frankl, Viktor. *Man's Search for Meaning*. Beacon Press, 2006.

61. Pipers, Watty. *The Little Engine That Could*. Platt & Munk: New York, 1930.

62. https://www.poetryfoundation.org/poems/42891/stopping-by-woods-on-a-snowy-evening

63. https://www.entrepreneur.com/article/197546

64. https://www.grandviewresearch.com/industry-analysis/frozen-food-market

65. https://www.statista.com/statistics/878354/fedex-express-total-average-daily-packages/

66. https://www.goodreads.com/author/quotes/101882.Calvin_Coolidge

67. https://archive.org/stream/brethrenevangeli78150bens/brethrenevangeli78150bens_djvu.txt ("In Your Face," unknown author, see pg. 13)

68. https://www.newreleasetoday.com/lyricsdetail.php?lyrics_id=38941

69. *Today in the Word*. Moody Bible Institute, January 1992, p. 8. (https://bible.org/node/13232)

70. Lewis, C.S. *God in the Dock*. Wm. B. Eerdmans: Grand Rapids, MI, 1972.

71. https://www.goodfight.org/articles/hollywood/steven-spielberg/

72. https://www.psychologytoday.com/us/blog/side-effects/201009/medicating-children-the-controversy-over-early-detection

73. https://winstonchurchill.org/resources/speeches/1941-
1945-war-leader/the-price-of-greatness-is-responsibility/

74. https://allianceforreligiousfreedom.com/educate-
yourself/quotes/presidents-quotes-on-the-bible/

75. Meynet, Roland. *A New Introduction to the Synoptic Gospels.*
Convivium Press, 2010. (https://www.goodreads.com/work/
quotes/6912791-a-new-introduction-to-the-synoptic-gospels)

76. medhealthdaily.com/symptoms-of-starvation

77. https://www.theatlantic.com/technology/archive/2018/05/
when-did-tv-watching-peak/561464/

78. Canfield, Jack. *Chicken Soup for the Christian Soul.* "The Bible", from Dear
Abby. Chicken Soup for the Soul Publishing LLC: Universal Press Syndicate, 2012.

79. https://allianceforreligiousfreedom.com/educate-
yourself/quotes/presidents-quotes-on-the-bible/

80. https://www.barna.com/research/the-bible-in-america-6-year-trends/

81. Ibid.

82. DailyCaller.com, 10/28/19.

83. https://www.thegospelcoalition.org/blogs/evangelical-history/why-
ben-franklin-called-for-prayer-at-the-constitutional-convention/

84. https://www.guideposts.org/faith-and-prayer/prayer-stories/
pray-effectively/6-ways-to-pray-like-abraham-lincoln

85. Ibid.

86. Bonnke, Reinhard. Hillsong Presents. Easter, 2013. (https://now.hillsongchannel.
com/hillsong-presents-reinhard-bonnke-1/season:1/videos/hd-hcspl1705)

87. https://www.biblestudytools.com/classics/moody-
anecdotes-illustrations/the-blood.html

88. Swift, James. "The Problem with Gore, Violence and Blood in Contemporary
Media". Thought Catalog, July 16, 2015. (ThoughtCatalog.com)

89. The Guttmacher Institute, https://www.guttmacher.org/united-states/abortion

90. https://www.biblestudytools.com/classics/moody-
anecdotes-illustrations/the-blood.html

91. https://www.hymnal.net/en/hymn/h/1006

92. Source: redcrossblood.org/donate-blood/hot-to-donate/
hot-blood-donations-help/blood-needs-blood-supply.html

93. https://www.sermoncentral.com/sermons/the-cross-of-christ-
steve-shepherd-sermon-on-cross-66260?ref=SermonSerps

94. Jones, Lewis E. There is Power in the Blood, 1899. (https://library.
timelesstruths.org/music/There_Is_Power_in_the_Blood/)